P9-DCD-001

TOWERS TO ETERNITY

By

DR. PAUL E. FREED

TRANS WORLD RADIO

CARY, N.C.

Sixth printing

Published in Nashville, Tennessee, by Thomas Nelson Inc., Publishers and simultaneously in Don Mills, Ontario, by Thomas Nelson & Sons (Canada) Limited. Manufactured in the United States of America.

Scripture quotations are from the King James Version of the Bible.

Library of Congress number: 79-2799

ISBN 0-8407-5709-3

This book is dedicated to Mildred Forsythe Freed and Ralph Freed, my godly parents, now with the Lord, whose selfless, loving yet uncompromising lives have been my greatest human inspiration.

And to my wife, Betty Jane, who has supported me faithfully in prayer and with loving deeds through the most extraordinary times of my life, since the founding of this ministry.

Dr. Paul E. Freed, Founder of TWR

CONTENTS

PREFACE

This is the story of Trans World Radio's beginning, which took place not at one of its station locations, but in the heart of one man, Paul E. Freed. The Lord knew how He would use Paul Freed for this great missionary venture and developed in him a keen missionary spirit while still a young boy growing up in the Middle East. His parents, who were missionaries for 27 years in what is today Syria, brought a depth of missionary vision to Paul's life that he would otherwise never have known.

Just as Trans World Radio had its beginning in the heart of one man, so today it has become the heartbeat of many men and women worldwide. Some of these dedicated workers are mentioned in the chapters of this book. Others, however, who have joined TWR's ministry since this writing, are likewise filling vital roles in propagating the work begun in 1952. They are the unseen, unheard-of people whose lives have been intertwined in TWR's ministry.

This book takes the reader through the initial stages of Trans World Radio's history, starting with "The Voice of Tangier," followed by the Monte Carlo station, and concludes with the construction of TWR's transmitting station on Bonaire. Since Bonaire, Trans World Radio has built broadcasting facilities or utilized existing stations around the world. With nearly 1,000 hours of programming every week being aired from the many transmitting sites, Trans World Radio has become a household word to many overseas listeners.

TWR has also established an international presence on five continents and one subcontinent. National partners—autonomous organizations responsible for translating, adapting, and producing most of TWR's programs into the languages of their people, as well as handling listeners' correspondence and follow-up—are located in more than 30 countries. Today, hundreds of thousands of letters are received each year from listeners tuning in to TWR's broadcasts; 25,000 to 40,000 letters arrive each month from India alone.

Where does Trans World Radio go from here? What new doors of opportunity will the Lord open in the future? We do not know, but one thing is certain, He is the same omnipotent God who planted the seed of this ministry in one man's heart many years ago. *Towers to Eternity* chronicles the events that came as a result of that seed flourishing and eventually blossoming into a worldwide broadcasting ministry for God's glory. May His name be praised.

A. L. Robertson, D.D.
Vice-Chairman of the Board of Directors,
Trans World Radio

CHAPTER I
A RELUCTANT AGENT

Never will I forget that muggy day in 1948 as I got off the train in Barcelona. I was NOT interested in Spain. I would much rather have gone almost any other place in the world than Spain. I did not know Spanish. I had no particular concern for the Spanish people. Spain was the most unlikely country for me—after an exciting childhood spent in Arab lands. And I had no idea what I was doing in Barcelona.

Outside the Moorish train station, I was ushered into some kind of contraption called a taxi. It was unlike any vehicle in which I had ever traveled, run by a charcoal burner on the back of it. The odor from the fumes was so bad I did not know whether I should hang my head out or suffer inside. It was not a good beginning.

The sight of the red and yellow flag of Spain, waving over the station, caught me wondering why God had led me this direction. Back in Winona Lake, Indiana, it had seemed logical enough that I should heed Torrey Johnson as he told me, "Paul Freed, I believe God would have you go to Europe."

Nothing was anticipated beyond the International Youth For Christ Conference in Beatenberg, Switzerland. I had been abroad earlier in my life, traveling between the States and my parents' mission field in Palestine and Syria. I was now thirty years old, married, and supposedly settled; but it seemed this was God's time for me to cross the Atlantic again, even though it was not easy to leave my wife in the States.

The international conference in Switzerland drew men from all over Europe as well as many from America. But the two zealous gentlemen who were delegates from Spain became God's important links in the chain of my personal destiny. They pleaded for someone to come back to Spain to help them bear the massive burden of reaching their 30,000,000 fellow countrymen with the Gospel.

Finally I had said I would go—a very puny, reluctant "yes"—but I was on my way. Little did I realize then that God was building the studding for my whole future work during those few days I was in Spain.

When I began to open my eyes, however, I was almost immediately captured by the rugged beauty of the mountainous peninsula. Even more I was drawn to the Spanish people—in the crowded cities, as I bounced over cobblestones that led to stone-fenced hamlets, as I peered into dark mountain cave homes. Wherever I went I began to be strangely stirred by the people of Spain.

Spain's civil guards, famed for iron discipline, policed the country roads in pairs. Andalusia's peasant men and women worked side by side in the olive groves. In the carefully tended orange groves, in the rice paddies up to their knees in water, in the shade of the front door—sewing, embroidering, making lace or fishing nets—all over the nation the people worked long and hard to gain a livelihood.

In caves hollowed out of soft rock along the high road above the Alhambra lived the gypsies, who have been in Spain so long that no one remembers exactly when they first appeared. But their dark good looks, flounced skirts, and spirited dances have become a part of the Spanish tradition.

Everywhere we went in Spain's rural areas we had people

politely offer us whatever they happened to be eating. I was informed that the correct answer is, "Thank you. May it do you good."

In one of the suburbs we saw serious-faced young men training for the dangerous bull-fighting profession. During the actual encounters, girls in mantillas graced the arena. At the sidewalk cafes little tables beckoned us to sit down while vendors circulated—selling shrimp, potato chips, crab mandibles, lottery tickets, and other things. In the elegant cafes, lit by great crystal chandeliers, the gentry in furs and diamonds dined.

A newcomer among the Spaniards, I found myself responding to their courtesy, their friendly inquisitiveness, their dignity, and their respect for human values. Perhaps it was the impact of all these qualities reaching out to me that created my profound response to the Spanish people. Along the city streets crowded with old women in black, selling chickens and figs and chestnuts and peppers, I heard the rattle of mule carts and wagons. I smelled the scent of orange blossoms and hot frying shrimp. I felt an inexplainable concern growing in my heart.

Through intricate iron lace gates I could see cattle barons, olive magnates, orange and cork kings sipping sherry, resting in cushioned chairs, far removed from the crowds in the street. Outside on the cobblestones the "other half" jostled me—farmers, shopkeepers, peasants, dockhands, beggars, gypsies, children, vendors—slight, agile people, knowing and cynical, yet so appealing to me with their dark eyes and sudden smiles.

Spain has a thousand faces. Some are harsh and lined with care, others are sunlit and gay. It is a land of hard-working, self-respecting peasants, of colorful gypsies, of tough soldiers, of artists and priests and merchants and noblemen. It is a land of geographic variety—snow-capped mountains, bare hills, fertile green fields, barren steppes, and sub-tropical coastal plains.

History too has left a variety of imprints across the country. The graceful arches of a Roman aqueduct have stood for twenty centuries. Assembled without mortar or cement, the granite stones fit together perfectly, and until just recently water still flowed through its conduit. Ruins and well-kept ancient structures all over the peninsula record footholds gained by the passing Romans, Visigoths, and Moors.

The Alhambra, sprawling fortress-palace completed during the fourteenth century by the Moors, remained the stronghold of African Moslems until Ferdinand and Isabella re-conquered Granada the same year Columbus sailed west with their blessing.

In Madrid the pace of daily life is sped up through many modern devices. In addition to her wide avenues fringed with skyscrapers, Madrid bears other marks which make her contemporary—neon lighting, underground stations, traffic jams, snack bars. Barcelona, on the Mediterranean, is so bustling with modern business and commerce that it is hard to comprehend that Julius Caesar once spent three years here!

Traveling out in the villages I was troubled by the little children who tugged at my coat in the streets. "*Tengo hambre!* I'm hungry!" Some in rags, some barefoot, some with no clothes at all—I'd never seen anything like it. I glanced into one face after another, reading obvious longing in their flashing eyes. I was disturbed by the sight of scrawny bodies, but I was absorbed by the realization that these little people needed the comfort, the protection, the love of the Lord. Through their tattered veil of poverty, even I—an unwilling stranger in their midst—could see the strength of a proud heritage. The Spaniard is an individualist, I was to learn. Philosopher Miguel de Unamuno wrote of his own countrymen, "It is difficult to govern a nation of twenty-two million kings."

Shortly after we arrived from Switzerland I attended my first church service. I was invited to a tiny upper room where I was asked to speak to the local Christians through an interpreter. As I started to speak, I studied their faces—so lined with need and difficulty, yet so warm with a hope that seemed tragically lacking out in the streets.

Great lumps rose in my throat as I said to these courageous people, "I can't tell you anything. Please, I don't want to speak to you. You tell me something. You know God in a way I don't know Him. Won't you please let me sit at your feet? I want to hear something from you."

There was a quiet looking from one to another among them. Finally, a silver-haired man stood and said, "If there's one thing that is true in our lives—it's that Jesus Christ means more than anything else to us."

There was no doubt about the fact that he meant what he said. I found myself crying out to God that He would mean that much to me.

The few hymnbooks and Bibles they owned had to be shared, but I have never seen Christian disciples anywhere such as I saw in Spain. And I wondered if God perhaps would have to send heaviness and difficulty to me before I could love Him as they did.

To be very candid, it seemed that what motivated me so strongly to help the Spanish Christians was the sturdiness of the believer I met wherever I visited—from the Pyrenees villages in the north, to sunny Andalusia on the Mediterranean. It seemed that God was asking me to help them multiply their spiritual blessings in order to reach others of their own people with a positive gospel message. I gradually realized that these people, in whom I had never had any personal interest, were burdened with needs equally as great as the Arab people I had grown up with and whom I had longed to serve.

I ranged from city to hamlet—largely to meet groups of Christians and to hold evangelistic services. The interest was keen wherever I went, and the whole time I was there, I never once spoke to an empty seat. In fact, often the chairs were removed to make room for more of the hungry of heart. No matter where I went the needs were urgent.

Faith in Jesus Christ was no casual commitment. He was the key to their buoyant courage. Someone had told me that Spaniards were made up of two parts—piety and gaiety. In Spanish Christians this was a winning combination that carried them through unbelievable circumstances. I had never seen anything like it. They loved Him with all their hearts, and after I had preached for two or three hours, they would ask, "Is that all? Can't you tell us more about the Lord Jesus Christ?"

One old woman I met out in a village was a wonderful Christian. I talked with her about the beauty of the morning and the loveliness of the Spanish countryside. Her comment was a rebuke to me, "Pablo, you're off the subject again. Why do you get off the subject? Why don't you talk to me about Jesus? I'd rather talk about Jesus than anything else."

Durable faith such as hers was contagious, too—the fellowship among Spanish Christians was no static tradition. Jesus Christ filled their lives to overflowing, and the love of God poured out to warm and convince others. When they came together, they often brought someone new with them—a neighbor, a friend, a relative, someone with a growing hunger for something permanent. I cannot remember ever speaking in Spain without someone new coming to the Lord.

The question, "How can more of them hear of the goodness of God?" disturbed my thoughts continually, as I woke with the crowing of the cock in the Andorran highlands, as I walked through the dim woods of the historic Alhambra and heard the rare notes of a nightingale. In the low-ceilinged cave dwellings sliced out of the arid steppes, in the stone-fenced shepherd hamlets, across the vast web of vineyards, through the silver-green sea of olive trees, I marched to the silent rhythm of a nation's cry for God.

Long after I returned to the comparative comfort of life in Greensboro, N. C., I was haunted by the heartbeat of a country where millions had never heard the real good news of Jesus Christ. The black-smocked miller, the gypsies, the muleteers, the matadors, the lace-mantillaed ladies, the ragged toddlers, the shoeshine boys, the shawled peasants—all of them wandered in and out, and back and forth over my inward eye. As I talked to Christian teen-agers, pleaded with middle-aged die-hards, prayed for wayward children and their deafened parents in America—a nation honey-combed with thousands of churches, I had to admit in the solitude before God: I am a captive to Spain and to her longing for the Living Lord.

The picture was so vivid, yet so complex. In the second most mountainous country in Europe, the Spanish terrain was intricately woven with hard-to-reach communities. Thirty million people tugged at my heart. There was only one answer in my mind to the problem. Radio. Like nothing else, radio could blanket the nation from peak to valley, from inland Madrid to coastal Cadiz. I did not have a dime of support, I did not know what steps to take. But one thing of which I was sure—the Lord had unquestionably linked my heart to the heart of Spain.

CHAPTER II
AN INNOCENT ABROAD

There was no doubt about it! Sharing the Gospel with millions of Spaniards would be no small task. There were times when I felt about as insignificant as I had one day years before out in the middle of the Atlantic Ocean. The voyage was taking me from Southampton in England to New York City. I was seventeen years old, and bored. Every inch of the *S. S. Queen Mary* was mine. There was no more territory to conquer after three long days on board. And the rails topside fenced me like prison bars.

Suddenly someone went by. A massive frame caught my idle attention, and I turned and started to follow the man around the deck. Suddenly he wheeled on me and demanded, "What do you want, boy?"

I was scared half to death, and I flushed a warm red all the way down as I stammered, "Well, I was just watchin' you!"

In the next second he went down in my book as a really great man. He deftly put me at ease as he countered, "Come on, walk *alongside* of me. You don't need to stay back there."

We talked about the ship, the weather, the ocean, people, sports. And we wound up in the recreation room playing table tennis. He was about the best ping-pong player I'd ever seen—

which began to make sense when I discovered that he was an Irish National Tennis Champion.

"If you want to come to my cabin," he suggested, "I'll show you something."

The boredom vanished as I walked beside him with a smug feeling of having made it with just about the most famous passenger on board!

When we got to his cabin he opened a suitcase, and pulled out a big iron ball with a chain on it. I recognized it as the kind you swing around the top of your head and let fly.

"I'm the world's Olympic champion hammer thrower," he said as he handed it to me.

I gulped.

He was so friendly to me. But he looked like a real mountain of a man, and I eyed him with open wonder. I was so proud to have made this kind of new friend. But the swagger drained out as I felt a Voice inside me saying,

"I want you to speak to this man. I want you to tell him about Jesus Christ."

I was terrified. Imagine an insignificant kid trying to tell this great world champion something. My first thought was to panic, "No, I can't. I just can't do it."

But the Voice inside was steady and calm. In spite of my fear to speak I was reaching in my pocket for the little New Testament I carried with me. I knew I would have to do the best I could even if it was pretty bad. I could at least read John 3:16 to him out of the Bible.

My voice sounded very far away—as though it were coming out from under one of the lifeboats.

"Excuse me, sir. I just wanted to read you something from this little book. I know you're a busy man, but . . ."

He watched as I read the old familiar words, "For God so loved the world, that He gave His only begotten Son, that whosoever believeth in Him should not perish, but have everlasting life."

There was no way of knowing how he would react. When I finished, he put his great big hand on my shoulder and said, "Thank you, son. You have no idea how much this means to me. I'm going to remember what you've said. And listen, buddy, don't you ever be afraid to do for other people what you just did for me."

Many times in my early life, I felt God was asking me to witness for Him. But as a boy I rationalized. I thought I couldn't do it. There must be some other way—through the preacher, through my parents, through the Sunday School class. But no, Lord, not through me individually. *I* can't do it.

But He never let me off the hook. God was continually bringing me back to the point of a personal testimony for Jesus Christ. This incident as a teenager on shipboard was an encouragement to me. The Lord firmly led me along to accept the importance of my telling others of His love.

And I knew without a doubt that His burden on my heart for Spain would eventually meet with the same encouragement. The mountain that loomed ahead would actually move if I would trust and not be afraid.

CHAPTER III
THE TWIG IS BENT

The guiding hand of God was threaded through my life in a pattern of "trust and obey" from my very earliest remembrance. My mother and father gave my sister and me the most wonderful home we could possibly have had.

Before I was born, they were attracted one day by a sign advertising special meetings, hanging in front of an old town hall down the road from the church where they attended. The pastor had warned his congregation, "Stay away from those fanatics!"

But Mildred and Ralph Freed were curious, and their subsequent conversion to Christ at the makeshift altar in a town hall changed the mainstream of all our lives.

My father was an official with the Burroughs Adding Machine Company in Detroit, Michigan. They employed 10,000 people in the home office alone, and as foreign service manager Father was in regular contact with the top executives.

God, however, had a different plan for all of us. And the road to Trans World Radio began one very ordinary morning in Father's office. This is how he tells the story:

"A man who worked with me at Burroughs—probably twenty years older than I—brought in the mail every morning. He had told me he belonged to a church; but he actually was sour and

Dr. Ralph and Mildred Freed in 1954

bitter against the things of God. He seemed to think a great deal of me—always called me 'Ralphie.' But often when I would witness to him he would say, 'Ralphie, you are too intelligent to believe this kind of stuff.'

"I wouldn't argue with him; I would just re-emphasize what the Lord had done for me. Then one morning in my office after we finished our business, he waited a minute before leaving.

" 'Something has been going through my mind, Ralphie. Will you promise me you will give me a straightforward answer? You have been talking to me about salvation—the blood of Christ. You've been trying to tell me there is no other way to God but through Jesus Christ. I believe there are a lot of ways to God, Ralphie. What about those people in Africa and the Orient and South America, and all those other places where they've never heard about Jesus Christ?'

"I answered him directly, 'Friend, I believe with all my heart that there is no salvation apart from Christ. The Bible says, "No man cometh to the Father but by me . . ." '

" 'Ralphie, do you mean what you say? If you really believe that all those people are lost without Jesus Christ, and are going to hell, as you put it, and you are satisfied here in your fine office, in this comfortable swivel chair, drawing your dependable salary, if all this is really true, then I say that you are the biggest hypocrite I have ever known in my whole life.'

"It was a tremendous blow to my pride. But I knew he was sincere, and that he respected me as a person. I thanked him and he left. When I went home that night I couldn't sleep, because I was thinking about all the implications of his confrontation. I was very happy at Burroughs, I had a wonderful wife, and a baby boy. And my present life looked successful as it rolled out before me with a promising future.

"But when I returned to the office the next morning, that office didn't look the same anymore. That swivel chair didn't seem to feel nearly so comfortable as it had the day before.

"A year and half went by before we made a move, but when we did we felt no uncertainty at all about the call of God to us for service among people who did not know the love of Jesus Christ in their lives."

* * * * *

When Father turned in his resignation, Burroughs offered to make him their sales manager over all of Europe. They figured he had some wanderlust that made the fields look greener over the sea. They thought he was asking for foreign service. The one thing they could *not* believe was that he wanted to leave Burroughs. They told him he could set up whatever organization he liked, do anything he felt needed doing. They offered him a carte blanche—he could write his own ticket. But Father thanked them and explained, "It isn't wanderlust driving me to new exotic places. It's God."

One of the head men shook his head and said, "Ralph Freed, if at any time you want to come back to Burroughs, we'll be glad to have you. Just send us a collect wire, and we'll work out a new arrangement for you—anytime; I mean *anytime* this thing gets too much for you, you're welcome to return to Burroughs."

There was a new baby sister, Ruth, just three months old by the time my parents uprooted the Birmingham, Michigan, home and moved to Nyack, New York, to attend the Missionary Training Institute. Using their savings, the first year in school went smoothly, but by the second year there was no capital left on which to live. I remember my father scrubbing floors, drawing maps, digging ditches—anything to keep the family going.

At one point the whole thing got to be almost too much, and Father recalled the Burroughs offer. The best he could do was not enough. The money was gone, and there was nothing to eat. Saturday morning, with the cupboard bare and no breakfast in our stomachs, we waited for the mail in hopes God would have moved some friend to send a small gift. There was no mail. Father had one nickel left.

Mother got us ready, and we all walked downtown, Ruthie in the baby carriage. When we came to the drugstore, Father pulled out his last nickel and placed it on the counter. He selected as large a candy bar as five cents could buy, and handed it to me. I was surprised to have candy offered to me in the middle of the day when I was supposed to be eating meat and potatoes, but I ate it.

Then as we passed the Western Union office, Father stopped, turned to Mother and said, "Mildred, you and I will be glad to do anything. But when our children are hungry, and we have nothing to give them—that is too much! I cannot go any further. I'm through trying to do what's impossible. I'm going to send a collect telegram to Burroughs."

Mother stalled for time, "Let's just think a minute, Ralph."

"No," Father insisted, as he started in the door. "We cannot go on like this. I'm going to send a wire right now."

I have never forgotten the gentle but firm love and faith that lit mother's face as she looked up at him, "Ralph, let's just prove God once more. Just one more time."

As we returned to the apartment they gave me the key and I ran ahead to open the door. I could hardly believe what I saw. The room was loaded with food. All over everywhere there were sacks of potatoes, pies, vegetables, meat, flour, sugar, cereal, chickens, bread—all the food anyone could possibly imagine on an empty stomach.

But this was no mirage! Mother and Father, coming in behind me, looked in amazement at each other and dropped to their knees to thank God. To this day we do not know who the delivery boy was. But we do know—GOD sent it.

More than anything else Mother and Father wanted to live to please God. He was central in every choice, every plan. That is why our home was so marvelous, no matter where it was—Detroit, Nyack, Jerusalem, Dera'a. We lived under a variety of conditions, but their relationship remained sure. They were in love to the end. Their real Christian attitudes toward each other and toward us as children taught us a great deal about living positively. There was nothing too big to discuss with us—on our own level, of course. Both my sister, Ruth, and I felt important, always a real part of our parents' lives. They always made us feel included in their decisions, their projects.

I might inject here that the gulf between young people and adults, children and parents, is a serious one in our country. Too often we say by our behaviour, "Well, they're still young; they shouldn't be bothered. This is too complex, too difficult for them—they should not be included." We have seen that Communism involves youth from a very early age. As I look back I believe that this one factor—being included as a rightful member of a basic situation—led me into missions as my life's work, rather than turning me against it. In fact, I feel very much that everything, as far as my life and ministry is concerned, is very closely related to what happened to me as a boy, a missionary child, with my parents.

Our family love and devotion kept us very close—not only Mother and Father, but also Ruth and me. She was, and still is, a wonderful sister. Ruth meant much to me, especially as children and teen-agers when we were away from our homeland, living among the Arabs. Later in college and Bible school, as we faced adjustments, she and I spent many happy hours discussing our joys as well as helping each other with the problems that are normal in the formative years of life.

Father's appointment in the Middle East as general area chairman with the Christian and Missionary Alliance led us to work among the people of Palestine, Transjordan and Syria. We were the only missionaries for 300 villages when we lived in the little town of Dera'a in the Hauran in southern Syria. As far as we were concerned our mission home was the "crossroads of the world." Arabs automatically dropped by the house at any time of the day, and we did everything we could think of to make them feel welcome.

My first experience of trying to lead a friend to Christ took place when I was about eight years old, right in our own backyard in Dera'a, a small town near the border of Arabia. An Arab boy, two or three years older than I, stopped at our house to say, "Lady, I'd like to work."

This was a new variety of boy to us, for working is not what the Arabs enjoy most. Mother told him we did not have any work for him, but he persisted, "Please Lady, I need a little work for just a few days."

He seemed so winsome that Mother finally relented and told him he could stay. His name was Thani, meaning second, second boy in his family. Arabs count only boys when reporting their children; for example, we have three children (boys) and two girls.

Thani and I struck up quite a friendship. Sometimes he did work, other times he had very different ideas. One day Mother was leaving for the village to buy meat. She took me along with her, and left Thani at home by himself. On our return trip, as we came close to the house, we heard terrible crying. Thani was inside, crying his heart out.

"It's so terrible—my head, my head," he wailed loudly.

His head was all wrapped up and it took us a while to get the whole story from him. Arab boys follow the custom of wearing their hair thick and long to protect their heads from the intense heat of the sun. Thani, it turned out, had decided that he wanted to be like me, so he had gotten Mother's shears, and given himself a haircut. He had cut and trimmed and chopped—there was a hunk out here and a hunk out there. He was a sight to behold! And all the time he kept crying, "Oh, I've been so bad!"

In between sobs we finally made out, "Lady, I thought while you were away I'd try to make your room look pretty. I thought maybe I could put some pretty designs on your wall."

Thani had gotten into some light blue paint, and had, indeed, put all kinds of designs everywhere.

"It looks terrible! I've ruined your house. And I've ruined my whole head. I feel awful! I've been a bad boy. Something's wrong in my heart."

I knew Mother was a real Christian, but the marks of love were outstanding that day as she put Thani at ease, "Don't cry about it, Thani. We will help you. We will help you fix it. Don't worry."

Finally when she had gotten his crying stopped, I wandered with Thani out into our little yard—only stones and dirt with a few chickens scratching around.

"My heart is so heavy," moaned Thani, "and I am so bad!"

I put my arm around him, and said, "You're no worse than I am. I've been just as bad as you many times. There's only One who can help us. That's Jesus. He can come into your heart and give you a new one just as He did for me."

And right there in my little chicken yard, I had the privilege of leading Thani to the Lord Jesus. A few days later Thani told my mother, "You don't know how happy I've been since Jesus came into my heart. But I've been thinking about my daddy and mother back in my village. They don't know Jesus. And my brothers and sisters don't know Him. And all of my friends back there, they've never heard of Him. I'm so happy about myself, but how about my people? I have to tell them about Jesus Christ. I have to go back to my village."

That night Thani wrapped up all his stuff in a great big kerchief. The next morning—with his bundle and a lunch—he joined a camel caravan that lumbered down the street right past our house, carrying wheat and grain to his village, thirty miles away in the Hauran.

My father had already begun a ministry there in Jebeib, the village where Thani lived, and the next time he headed for that village he took me with him. Several weeks had elapsed between the day Thani traipsed down the road in the caravan and our arrival in Jebeib in the old Model A Ford. We parked at the edge of the village and walked into town through the narrow, rutted streets. After the usual greetings, two or three of the village leaders began talking with us about Thani: "This boy who has come back from your place is so different. He's such a good boy now and he lives right, and all the time he talks about Jesus Christ."

Thani was the main entrance for the Gospel to the people in Jebeib, and his testimony was a moving factor in the foundation of a Christian church in his village. He experienced the love of God in our home, then went out of our circle of love to share what he had found with those he loved back home. God had taken up residence in a little boy's heart and life, and everybody could see the difference. My basic emphasis on evangelism today goes directly back to Thani. He was the first to awaken my personal concern for the needs of other people. He was the first one to show me the change that the power of God makes in a person.

A trip with my father into a village was the greatest news that could break for me in those days when we were stationed off in the hinterland of Syria. A pioneer spirit seemed to lead me away from the reasonable comforts of home, driving me to recognize that missionary work is meeting the needs of individuals wherever they are.

The boys of the villages would always flock around the car, and it was my job to guard it while Father was occupied talking with the men and women. The kids were not mean, but they were full of boyish instinct. And in ignorance and curiosity they could end up doing a lot of damage—like picking up sharp stones and writing on the shiny surface of the car. For a while we felt terrible about the arithmetic problems and penmanship exercises that were scratched all over our automobile, but Father learned that the finish of the car was expendable, as long as we could run the car to carry the Gospel to the villagers.

The car became an early vehicle of learning as well as transportation for me. Arab boys admired Americans and were eager to find out more about us and our high-powered machines. It was through these informative conversations around the car that I picked up a local vocabulary and was eventually able to speak Arabic well enough to talk with boys about Jesus Christ. By the time we were ready to leave a village there would often be as many as twenty Arab children hanging on the car! Running boards, bumpers, hood, fenders, all were full. If we failed to shoo them off, we would give them an exciting ride—picking up speed until they would ask us to stop and let them off because they were getting so far from home.

Adventures such as these built into my childhood the framing for later contacts with people, and I grew up sharing my parents' work, and realizing more and more of what constitutes a meaningful Gospel ministry for needy people in pioneer areas.

Often for a trip of several days' duration we would equip the car for camping so we could do our own cooking. Our checklist of about seventy-five items included matches, pressure cooker, kerosene, water, and many other necessities. This kind of journey gave me opportunities to practice Arab customs such as shooting with a camel's hair slingshot or drinking from a clay pitcher.

Every Arab home places a pitcher of water by the door for the refreshment of those who pass by. Since their method of drinking requires skilled pouring from a spout far above the mouth, the vessel remains at least reasonably sanitary for all who are thirsty. You can imagine, however, the wet, hilarious rehearsals we went through before we became proficient at the art of long-distance drinking.

The Arab boys taught me to use the same kind of sling that David used to kill the giant Goliath. He was no little boy with a toy, we discovered. The old Palestinian sling is a real weapon, using stones nearly the size of chicken eggs for fighting. They can be slung with great accuracy more than 100 yards. The slings are made of camel's hair, tightly woven to about a three-foot length. The "cup," also woven, is as large as a man's hand. We would place a stone in the middle of the braided hair strap, then wind it over our heads, and let it go with a terrific snap that sounded like the crack of a whip. Running three or four steps with it before we let it fly would add greater impetus, of course. I thought using it was great sport, especially when I got to the point where I could hit a telephone pole quite regularly at a distance of 50-75 yards.

Sometimes we would be invited to stay overnight when we had not come prepared. The Arabs are hospitable people, and their accommodations are simple. I experienced real joy in living with the natives, eating their food, sleeping on the floor, even though the floors were generally flea-infested. Often the animals share the house with the family.

When any stranger arrives it is normal for the Arab villagers to want to hear what he has to say. Our host would invite the neighbors to come in for coffee. This is a bitter, thick, black brew, beat by hand with a long bat-like stick in a wooden container. The chief, with his long black beard dangling in the cup, would take the first drink, then pass it to us. We knew we would have to drink, too, to show him we accepted his hospitality.

All of them are curious about a newcomer, and gathering together around the little fire at the close of the day offers good diversion from working in the fields. They would ask questions and my father would talk. More than any other way I remember my father sitting in the firelight in Arab headgear, telling the villagers of Jesus Christ—and really reaching them.

Later as I felt the burden for Spain growing on my heart, I relived some of these events in Arab lands which initiated my concern for the lost. Even back in those days I felt the limitations of witnessing to ones and twos. We could reach only a few in person as we sat about the fire in the village. And the question started to shape in my mind, "What about all the others who have never had a chance?"

Occasionally there was resentment among the Arab listeners, but more often, they showed real openness. Those who did understand and gave themselves to the Lord altered their whole pattern of living. Seeing them change from death to life through the power of the Gospel made such an impression on me that I will never forget it. So many things changed—lying, cheating, stealing, polygamy.

Father never argued with them about their sinful practices. He presented to them the joy and blessedness of turning themselves over to the Lord. He found "offerings" a touchy subject, however, at first. As the Lord established little groups of believers here and there, he began to feel that it was time to speak to them about the rewards of giving. It bothered him that the total monthly income for most of the Christians, in money and in goods, amounted to little more than ten dollars per family. They lived on plain bread, with a bit of sour milk and a bit of olive oil, in which they dipped the bread. Meat? Why just a piece of mutton was a Christmas feast! Father would ask us, "Now, how am I going to ask people like these to give to the Lord?"

His great desire was for them to give out of hearts full of love for Jesus Christ—to give liberally as an expression of their hearts' devotion.

One time when he was still learning the language, a young and very consecrated Arab was interpreting. In the course of his message, Father got into the subject of giving an offering and the Arab turned to him and said in English, "But Brother Freed, you mustn't do a thing like this to these people."

"Just go on," Father urged.

"But these people eke out a bare existence. How can you, an American—with all the money you people have, ask these people to give money?"

It was obvious that he was not going to translate any further. So Father just told him, "We'll discuss it later."

Weeks and months of talking and praying with this young Arab Christian followed the incident before he was convinced that this tangible expression of love was a basic teaching of the New Testament. He finally accepted the fact that giving, joyful giving, sacrificial giving, is a ministry, a privilege of the believer. He even became convinced that it is not so much a giving of what can be

Dr. Ralph Freed, general director of TWR, 1952–1973

easily spared that counts, but that God is proving us and our love for Him through a material measure—no matter what our financial standing.

In our home we were very sure that the Lord made up for all of our tithes and offerings—even when it was most difficult to pay it—not only in material ways, but in many ways. Father was concerned about the Arabs because he honestly believed he would be doing the poor farmers an injustice, as good believers, if he did not teach them this principle of giving. And he was right. We saw continuous evidence of the fact that when Jesus Christ comes into a person's heart, one of the signs is the opening up of his purse.

As they grew in the love and grace of the Saviour, we delighted in observing real love feasts with these Christian farmers during harvest time. On the threshing floor they would build up two piles—nine measures for their own use and one measure pressed down and running over for the Lord. It was a genuine testimony to what He was doing for them as they took "the Lord's pile" over to the little meeting house and poured it out on the floor. As a result of this joyous giving, they were able to send out evangelists into neighboring towns to preach the Gospel. These believers became known throughout the Arab world as the most outstanding example of sacrificial giving by the poorest of people. They were an inspiration to missionaries in other places who came to see, or heard about, the deep revival among our Arab farmers.

The effectiveness of my parents' ministry is very likely directly traceable to Mother's prayer life. She was always a step ahead of the rest of us in her devotion and faithfulness. How much of her time she spent praying for Father and for us children we will never know. Her favorite verse, "The steps of a good man are ordered of the Lord," was built into her prayer life. But that verse was always personalized by her postscript, "Lord, make Ralph that good man. Or Paul. Or Ruth." She was always confident that her Heavenly Father was taking care of us. Her manner of talking with Him was most simple and heartfelt. She did not care what anyone thought, she just talked—like we would talk with her—a comfortable conversation. She always believed in bringing everything down to a minimum equation.

"We have a prayer-hearing and prayer-answering God; and we come to Him through Jesus Christ. It's just that simple," she would say. "If God does hear prayer, and God does answer prayer, and God is the omnipotent One, then we should just go to Him and ask Him."

One of my happiest memories of childhood has to do with Mother and Father's belief in prayer and fasting. Friday, late afternoon and evening, was set aside in their week for this purpose. But I suppose the thing that impressed me most as a child was that Ruth and I never felt that we had to fast with them. In fact, Mother would go out of her way on pray-and-fast night to prepare for us the most wonderful meal of all. She often let us decide what we would like most for Friday supper. It must have been a real temptation for her as she prepared hot breads or cinnamon rice, and as the kitchen was filled with delicious smells on the evenings when she ate nothing. This evidence of love, plus their allowing us rather than forcing us to do as they did, stimulated our growth in grace, our desire to learn to walk with the One whom our parents followed closely. To this day I associate prayer and fasting with an unforgettable time of enjoyment.

Cinnamon rice on pray-and-fast nights, talks around an Arab fire, camel hair slings, and clay drinking pots all accumulated in my young mind to lead me to personal reliance on our Saviour, and a compulsion in my mind and heart to share Him with others. My evangelistic drive was to undergo a refining and maturing, but it never swerved from the main course set during my childhood. My greatest heritage was the life of my parents which demonstrated the Lord Jesus Christ to me through the everyday evidences of their love. All of our early life together laid the foundation for my personal commitment to Christ.

The story we will tell throughout the book of God's miracles in the establishment of our radio ministry can be understood only in the light of these influences that molded my life as a child.

CHAPTER IV
THE MAN IS FORMED

The ties that bound me so closely to my parents, however, also formed a web of chronic homesickness that entangled me during my school days away from home. One of the greatest difficulties for a family living outside its homeland is the separation that often becomes a by-product of good education for the children.

Moving from one mission station to another, from foreign service to furlough home, threw us into a variety of educational set-ups. We attended English and German schools in Jerusalem, and an American community school in Beirut. There were some grades when Mother became the teacher, and others when she selected a tutor to take over our academic training.

When I arrived in Wheaton, Illinois, to enroll at the Academy for high school studies there, they accepted me as a sophomore even though I never had been a freshman anyplace. But to get to the reasoning behind their decision in Wheaton, the road leads back to Bethlehem.

On even further back to Jerusalem, where I had been sent—at the critical age of eleven—to live in the mission home with two single lady missionaries. How could anything be worse—just as I was becoming aware of my masculine pride—than to be closeted all alone in the compound with two strange women?

The allowance which my parents sent me regularly from Dera'a diminished rapidly as I made daily trips to the postal station and to the telegraph office. Letters—written to my parents—evidenced undying hope that I might come home to live with them again. Telegrams were cryptic pleas to Father to rescue me from a situation I felt I could no longer bear.

Undoubtedly the ladies in the mission station were no happier than I about the arrangement which Mr. Freed had made with them for the care of his young son. I do not think they had ever had any previous experience in mothering homesick boys, but they had very firm ideas about what I should do. I do not know if it made them feel more successful to be hard on me constantly; but I do know that they succeeded in keeping me in a constant state of misery.

The older of the two, who officially had charge of my welfare, decided one day that I had not been taking adequate baths. She also made the dangerous decision that—since I was not to be trusted to clean up myself—she would have to give me a bath.

"You aren't gonna give me a bath!" I yelled.

"Oh, yes I am," Miss D— insisted.

About that time, Miss L—, younger, but just as determined—came into the room to strengthen the advancing enemy force.

"Paul Freed," she warned, "I want you to know that I'm going to stand behind Miss D—. And I'm going to see to it, too, that you get a bath!"

When she came at me with a broom, I bolted. Past her in a flash, I leaped the stairs in a single bound, cleared the front door, and kept on going out into the high-walled street. When I glanced over my shoulder, Miss L— was padding after me, waving the broom over her head. Arabs in the Street of the Prophets ducked as the chase continued, staring after us in wonder and amusement as I circled back to the mission compound and climbed over the wall.

She was right after me, making violent sweeps with the broom. I leaped from the wall on one side, ran across the courtyard, and clambered up the wall on the other side. And Miss L— was just barely missing me all the time.

Finally, she called out between gasps for breath, "All right, let's talk about it."

I have no recollection of the conversation. But I do know I took my own bath.

My parents tried to understand how very difficult those days were for me, and eventually allowed me to return to Dera'a to be with them for a time. But education pursued me relentlessly, and soon I found myself living in Bethlehem in a mission home with Mrs. Bernice Gibson and her two children. This was a better situation, for besides her daughter and son, there were also other missionary children living there, for whom she acted as house-mother. But I was still homesick.

When I turned thirteen they moved the mission home to the outskirts of Jerusalem. For some reason I ended up being the only boy in the group which in my young mind made the situation intolerable. My decision was a desperate, but bold one.

One night I wrote a note to the missionary in charge. Then before daybreak I tiptoed out of the house and joined a caravan into the center of Jerusalem. After cabling my father to ask him to meet me in Tiberias, Galilee, I found a public car headed north. All the way up I wondered what his reaction would be, but my heart flipped with joy when I saw his beloved face in the crowd as we pulled into the center of Tiberias. He tried to persuade me of my wrongdoing, but I can still remember how right I felt as I tried to explain. "Father, I left them a note. They know by now that I'm on my way home. I don't hold anything against them. I'm just terribly, terribly homesick. Can't I please come home, Father?"

He was concerned for my education but he finally said he would let me stay home if I would promise to work hard.

I never worked so hard in my life, in any formal school situation, as I did during that next year at home. I did my whole freshman year alone, writing long books. I did one on the countries through which we traveled in Europe—the history, geography, government, sociology, customs—everything I could possibly find out went into the narrative. Then I went through piles of travel folders and magazines to find pictures to illustrate my book.

When we pulled into Wheaton, Illinois, and headed for Wheaton Academy I lugged my books along with me. The admissions officer studied them seriously, decided they were worth several units of credit, and assigned me to the sophomore class.

Following that furlough year my parents returned with Ruth and me to the Middle East. This time I was sent to Beirut, Lebanon, where I was graduated from the American Community School, founded by faculty members from the American University in Beirut. There were only 100 students in the entire school, and three of us comprised the graduation class.

One of the other class members, Philip Freidinger, and I had become fast friends. He was the son of Presbyterian missionaries in Lebanon. After building our lives so closely together during our junior and senior years—sailing, biking, picnicking, talking, praying together—we decided to go on together to Wheaton College. This had been my plan all along, but it represented a rather significant switch for Phil, who had already been accepted at Oberlin College in Ohio.

In the summer of 1936 Phil and I left our parents in Beirut and set out for Wheaton. A month in the Swiss Alps and a bicycle tour through England gave us a head start on the education that waited for us at Wheaton College.

We moved into the same private home near the campus and I immediately won a reputation with the house parents for being lazy. I didn't take the usual kind of campus jobs which were fine for most students, but did not seem right for me. While Philip was working in the dining hall, I was selling flower cards and other Palestinian crafts to the residents of Wheaton and nearby suburbs. I was very fond of Philip, but I found a most depressing situation. I could never do anything right. Everytime I would do something I would get knocked down with, "Why don't you do it like Philip does it?"

The other home, where I lived later, conveyed a very different attitude. Mrs. Stevens, a widow, knew how to listen to us boys and to enter into constructive fellowship with us, by action as well as word. She and her son, Earle, were people touched by the love of God and creatively dedicated to extending His love to others by attitudes and everyday living. Each one of us was important and appreciated for himself. This allowed us to be free to expand, to serve, to learn.

There was all the difference in the world between the two climates. And I sensed that if I was to concern myself through life with the needs of human beings I would accomplish precisely nothing unless I was willing to care sacrificially.

The four years at Wheaton were full ones. My interest in people funneled me into an anthropology major, but there was nothing during my campus days that hinted a career in missionary radio would become my life's work.

The financial picture was a continual surprise. My parents kept in touch with me with a ten dollar monthly allowance, which of course did not cover very much. I never was quite sure how the college bills would be paid. Our following after God through the years had led us into a life of simple trust—like the lilies of the field, rather than into the comfortable security of a bank account.

One summer I spent in Gary, Indiana, working in the steel mill—on the swing shift, because it paid better. The money I earned I had scrupulously planned to put away for the next fall's tuition. However, an extremely serious infection not only laid me off the job several weeks but also required expensive hospitalization which used up every penny I had earned. At the end of the summer I hitchhiked back to Wheaton with no money at all for the year ahead.

All was fine until I reached the financial desk in the registration line. I asked for the most liberal terms possible, and was told they could not allow me to complete my registration without a deposit of one hundred dollars. My parents were a third of the way around the world. I had worked as hard as I knew how all summer long. I felt positive that I should go on in my college training. I needed one hundred dollars and I didn't have one cent. I had no idea where to turn.

Someone cheerfully suggested that I should drop out and work for a semester. I walked out of the registration line in the middle of the day, and it was like stepping into the black of midnight. I had never been so depressed in my life.

"Lord!" I cried. "You surely know best. What do You want me to do?"

As I walked through the halls and across the campus, people said, "Hi, Paul." But I was drowning in the busy sea of my own despair, and I recognized no one. Nothing had any meaning.

After an hour of aimless wandering, I decided the only thing I could do was to go back to work at the steel mill. I thought I had better find a bite to eat before I started out, but I felt so badly I did not know whether I would be able to swallow.

Suddenly out of the sodden blur of faces and sounds I heard my name, "Hey, Paul Freed, haven't you heard them paging you? Someone wants to get in touch with you."

When I went to the registrar's office, Dr. Enoch Dyrness spoke to me, "Paul, I understand you're planning to register. I have a little something here that should be of interest to you. There's been an anonymous gift sent in for your account. It's a check for one hundred dollars."

My mouth dropped open and I felt the tears smart under my eyelids. I saw again the apartment in Nyack with groceries piled all over the floor and the chairs and the tables. Dr. Dyrness could not possibly know all that went through my mind as he smiled and said, "Isn't that the way God works?"

Several years later I found out who sent it. A missionary in China had heard about me, through some of the other students at

Wheaton. One day my name kept coming to him. God seemed to be saying, "You should help Paul Freed." When he wasn't able to shake the thought he obeyed it, and from the very little that he had he took one hundred dollars and mailed it to me. God brought it 10,000 miles in time to check my desperation. If it had arrived one day later, I would have already been on my way back to the steel mills.

Besides other summer work—one year at the Pontiac Motor Company in Michigan, and another as business manager of a Bible Lands Tour—I started a small novelty belt business of my own. I had found it getting harder and harder to work for other people and make my income balance my outgo. Something else had to be done. So I began designing belts out of unusual materials.

In Chicago I located companies that would cut little uniform pieces out of nutshells, wood, cork, plastic, metal, leather. With a supply of thongs and heavy colored cord, I began all by myself to make belts right at the kitchen table. After getting so many orders I did not know what to do with them, I looked around for help. Other students who wanted piecemeal work later joined me at the going campus wage until we took over the whole second story of a house in Wheaton. First we marketed our novelty product through variety stores. But we discovered shortly that we could not sell them in sufficient quantities for that market to pay off.

I went to New York City and approached the J. C. Penney Company. The particular buyer who talked with me was one of the finest men I have ever met. He was so intrigued with my story that he committed the company to trying a few belt samples. They sold so well that we ended up with more orders than we could handle. From then on we sold many tens of thousands of belts exclusively through the 1600 stores of J. C. Penney.

The work continued in Wheaton for two more years, and the profits from the DuPage Craft Company's novelty belts not only put me through college and Missionary Training Institute too, but it helped several other students as well to make ends meet.

It was the fall of 1942 when I enrolled at Nyack—the same school my father had attended almost twenty years earlier. My further study in Nyack, New York, came comparatively easily, and I completed the three year course at the Missionary College in two years.

I have always been interested in missions, but there is no doubt in my mind that my later activities were greatly influenced by the missionary fervor there at Nyack. Overlooking the Hudson River, the school—which is the oldest Bible College in North America—is affectionately known by its alumni as the "mount of prayer and blessing."

During my stay on campus I learned about missions directly from missionaries, fresh from their fields of service, and much about the Word of God through systematic Bible study. Though I did not fully appreciate it at the time, I know now the Lord was speaking to me about the "regions beyond" through the lips and lives of godly teachers such as Dr. Harold Boon, the Reverend Gilbert Johnson, and Dr. Thomas Moseley; and through missionary statesmen such as Samuel Zwemer, authority on the Moslem world, and Clarence Jones, missionary radio pioneer from HCJB in Quito, Ecuador.

Along with my studying I opened a couple of churches, ran the belt business which was still headquartered in Wheaton, Illinois, and took additional courses at Columbia University.

The Christmas before graduation launched a series of introductions which was to affect the rest of my life. Some of us wanted to do something different but we did not know where to go. In the bull session that developed we decided we would buy and fix up for sale a half dozen Model A Fords, and drive them south. We got together as many gas ration stamps as we could, then we mixed an original formula for fuel, using cleaning fluid—and I forget what all—and drove as far as Durham, North Carolina. All of the cars sold on the auction block and our vacation was made.

For some reason I had enough before the other fellows, so I went on back to Nyack; but Eugene Evans, my roommate, stayed on a

Dr. Paul and Betty Jane Freed

couple more days. When he returned he let me have it immediately, "You really missed it, Paul. We went to a church Christmas party, and met a lot of interesting people. You should have been there. I met Clarence's girl friend. And is she something! You really should have stayed. She is really something. She is exactly the kind of girl you have always talked about!"

I was not interested. "I don't know why you're telling me about somebody else's girl friend!"

I had been dating different girls casually but nothing serious had developed. But Gene Evans would not drop the subject of this girl that he had met in Durham. I objected, "Gene, I wish you'd keep still. Why do you have to keep bothering me about a girl who's already going with one of our buddies?"

"Well, I think she's really something," he repeated.

"Will you please shut up?" I demanded heatedly.

But Gene was not finished. He took a long breath and kept going, "All I can tell you, Freedly, is that I've had to put up with you for two years here at school, and I know your tastes, and I know the kind of girl you would like, and I want you to listen to me now if you never listen again. She is it! I am absolutely certain that she is the girl for you. If you'd ever meet her I'm sure you'd agree in a minute!"

I cooled a bit and retorted, "Well, Gene, let's say she is it. I think you're crazy to try to tell me such an important thing on such flimsy evidence. I don't think you have any sense whatsoever. But even if she really is it, she's still going with Clarence. And he's my friend, too. And I've got no intention of beating him out of a girl I've never even laid eyes on!"

He remained adamant, "I don't care who she's going with now. They're just dating anyhow. And I've met her. And I know she's it!"

After a few days he quieted down and I forgot the whole conversation. Several months passed and it was time for graduation. It was the very last morning at school. I was in the post office checking my mail. A girl I knew stood by the door reading a letter. As we were exchanging goodbyes, she commented that she had just gotten a letter from her brother's girl friend in Durham, N. C. Something clicked in my mind. This was Clarence's sister; her brother was the one who had been dating the girl my roommate told me about at Christmastime. I leaned close enough to glance at the envelope in her hand. Sure enough. There it was—the same name my roommate had mentioned so insistently last winter, Betty Jane Seawell.

Without giving it any thought, I heard myself ask, "How about tearing off that flap for me, Eva?"

Just as spontaneously she tore it from the envelope and handed it to me. I tucked it into my wallet and forgot it.

CHAPTER V
A LETTER TO A GIRL

During the summer I moved to Greenville, S. C. to establish a church. I had just about completed a year there when one day I was cleaning out my billfold. I unfolded a discolored triangular envelope flap, and was about to toss it in the wastebasket when I remembered the chain of conversation eighteen months earlier. On an impulse I decided to do something I had never done—write a letter to this name on the faded old paper.

I do not remember ever having just written a letter to a girl. I always had the feeling we should enjoy the people we are with, and not be off in a corner trying to contact the people we cannot see. My current philosophy seemed to be: enjoy people when you are with them, and when you are no longer together, enjoy the new people at hand. You can see, I never was much for letter writing.

In fact, I never would have even kept this paper if Gene Evans had not made such a fuss about her! Now I did not know what to say to her. It was all so very crazy! I had never met her, never even seen her. And here I was trying to compose a sensible-sounding letter to a girl my roommate had met one night a year and a half before. I did not even know what her present situation was. It seemed like an insane thing to do. But I went through with it anyhow.

In three weeks I was to attend a pastors' conference not too far from her hometown. So I asked in the letter if I might stop by and meet her since she was a casual friend of my roommate in Nyack.

I did not get an answer, and I was undecided whether I should take the train directly to the conference, or drive my car so I could go by way of her home in Carthage. The last morning I was all packed. I left my car in a parking lot and walked down to the post office to check my mail. There was no letter. I had my suitcase with me, and I headed toward the train station. Suddenly I was stopped by a man who said, "Mr. Freed, I've got to talk with you. I have some terrible problems." I knew him only by sight. I smiled and said, "Well, I'll be praying for you."

"No," he explained, "It's more important than that. You've got to help me now. I'm in trouble."

"I'm sorry, but my train is due at 10:30, and I'll miss it if I stop to talk with you now. Let's make an appointment for next week when I come back?"

The man looked grim. "I don't know what to say to you. I'm sure your train is very important. But I can't imagine that your train—no matter where it's taking you—could be as urgent as what I have to have help with. Can't you understand? Life has come to an end for me. I'm through. My life is hopeless. There's no way out. I've got to have help."

I was getting as distraught as he by this time, "But I'm catching a train . . ."

"I've got to have help."

"Maybe someone else can help you."

"No, I just—" he stopped and began again. "You—you are the one who has to help me!"

"You mean you'd even make me miss my train?"

"Yes! Can't you understand? I've got to have help. And I want you to go with me right now and help me."

I picked up my suitcase, took him by the elbow, and turned back toward the lot where I had left my car.

"Well—if it's really that vital, I guess I have no choice. I'll do what I can to help you."

I took him across town to my church. It was really a converted store building, but it had been beautifully done inside. The benches we had made ourselves. The lighting was indirect and soft. The floor was all carpeted. We walked in and sat down. And he began to pour out his story of how alcohol had finally gotten the best of him.

"I'm through. There's no more reason to try to keep living. I've got a wonderful wife. But she says she can't stand me any longer. She's through with me. She's tolerated me as long as possible, and I don't blame her. I come in drunk, and I knock the children around. They're scared of me. They're hungry. And I'm no good to anybody. My wife said to me, 'You get out, and you get out for good. I'm through with you.' As a matter of fact, I'm through with myself. I'm just trying to figure out how to end it all."

I told him that there really was a God who loved him in spite of his horrible mess, that Jesus Christ could change his whole life. The Holy Spirit was there ahead of me that morning, and in the backwash of that man's hopeless confession there came the quiet assurance of the love and forgiveness of God. To the glory of God I want to say that the man was wonderfully saved. Together we prayed that God would change the pattern of ruin in his life.

I took him home to his family after we got through talking and praying and his wife listened while he told her what had happened. "This is the most wonderful thing I have ever heard," she said, and she too gave her heart to the Lord Jesus. The tears were running down both their cheeks as they held each other and she said, "By all means, if he means business I want him back. I want our home to be reunited more than anything else!"

Several days later, when I returned from North Carolina, I found the man had had a genuine experience of salvation. He had meant business with God. He had given up his drinking. Their lovely Christian home continues as evidence that it was worth missing the train that morning in August 1945—even though I was so stubborn about doing it. It was God's timing, and I almost stopped His clock!

After I left their home I drove back past the post office. This time there was mail in my box, and one of the letters was from Betty Jane Seawell, the girl on the envelope flap! It was a cool little note that said, "My parents will be glad to receive you . . ."

So I headed for Carthage. From the moment I stopped at the house and saw Betty Jane coming to greet me, I knew that Gene Evans was right. I might add that if I had not received the letter from her that morning, I would not have tried again to make a contact.

It was V-J day, and the world was rejoicing over the end of World War II. We had heard on the news that there would be two national holidays. Mr. Seawell was sure this turn of events would change the plans for the conference, so he insisted I use his phone to check before I took off again. He was right. The whole conference was called off, so I decided to head on back south.

Betty Jane's father stopped me with, "Oh no! You've had a long drive up here, young man. You just better spend the holidays with us before you turn around and go back."

I immediately sensed here were Christians with a strong testimony for Jesus Christ. Mr. Seawell is an outstanding Christian attorney gifted with a deep knowledge of the Bible as well as unusual wit both in speaking and writing which he uses constantly for the Lord. Mrs. Seawell, who went to be with the Lord October 5, 1965, was a talented Bible teacher who never failed to testify and to take a stand for the Lord Jesus Christ. People would often say, "When Jane Seawell talks to you she is sure to talk about her Lord and Saviour Jesus Christ." Today in Carthage, North Carolina, the Gospel Chapel is a monument to the faithful and untiring testimony of Chub and Jane Seawell—Mom and Pop to me.

At the time I stayed over in Carthage I do not suppose the

Seawells had any idea how important one day would be to Betty Jane and me. But when we were married, just seven weeks later, it was obvious to everyone that not only every day, but every hour, had been loaded with God's working out His plan for Betty Jane and me.

We could not get over how the Lord had been keeping us for each other. How vividly He had brought us into an experience of sureness—made our love so real, so deep, so honest and unselfish. How patiently He had cared for her until I was ready to listen.

"I maintain," Betty Jane tells people with a sparkle in her brown eyes, "that God had this man for me all the time. I want the same complete assurance for other young people. I really believe that they should trust that the Lord does have His exact choice of a mate for them, and that they'll only mess up their lives if they run ahead of the Lord and marry ahead of His schedule. And if there isn't someone in His plan, they're better off *not* marrying."

Betty Jane is always concerned about sharing our story correctly with young people, because we both feel that a considerably longer period of time is usually necessary for the laying of a sound foundation for marriage. Ours is no pattern to copy lightly. In our case there was really no reason to wait. Both of us had completed our education. I had been able to save enough money. We were both sure that God had moved us toward each other, and that our marriage was His plan.

CHAPTER VI
QUEST FOR A CAUSE

Early in the life of the Youth For Christ movement I left the pastorate to become YFC director in Greensboro, N. C. Torrey Johnson, founder of the new rally concept for high schoolers, fit my image of a leader who could clearly see the needs of others, then intelligently go about finding an appropriate plan of action to fill the need.

It was Torrey Johnson who taught me, not only to envision a new concept, but to move ahead in faith to accomplish the thing that appeared so inspired in a moment of clarity. It was Torrey who looked me straight in the eye at the Winona Lake, Indiana, conference and said, "Paul, I believe God would have you go to Europe." He pressed me to make the decision to attend the Youth For Christ conference in Beatenberg, Switzerland. Later I learned he had prepared my wife by telling her, "I don't think you should just let Paul go to Europe, I think you should urge him to go."

It was difficult to leave Betty Jane for we had been together almost constantly during the first three years of our marriage. The separation, however, proved constructive in both our lives. During her stay with my parents in their missionary cottage in Nyack she wrote to me about my mother:

"I've heard you tell how Mother has made a practice of praying two hours and twenty minutes each day. I couldn't understand how anyone could tithe his time for prayer! . . . I have never seen anyone live more perfectly than Mother does. She has a knack of doing her dusting, planning her meals, doing her cooking. She always looks neat and clean. Always seems rested, never cross or irritable. Always she's loving. To me she's a living example of what I would like to be when I think about following the Lord. I've wished I could see how it can actually be done, how some human being could actually put Christianity into practice. Well, darling, you've given me the opportunity! She is the epitome of a Christian. It's just like being 'oiled.' Her life moves without friction. I suppose it is the 'oil of the Holy Spirit.'

"Her desire is to be like Christ. It's not how much time she puts in—although she does keep close track in a little notebook of the time she spends praying. But I never have the feeling she's grinding it out. She's a very disciplined person, but not in a rigorous sense. She's just learned that when she works according to God's rules, life—like a well-tuned machine—runs smoothly. I miss you terribly, honey, but I thank you for this time of learning. It is good to be here with Mother and Father Freed."

Torrey probably had no hint that in urging me to go to Europe he was in a sense assisting God in pushing me right out of his popular new American youth organization. Neither had I any intention of leaving him. Nevertheless, on my return from Switzerland and Spain, I had a broadened comprehension of a world without hope.

In the Youth For Christ rallies I tried to share the acute burden I felt, and the vision that remained vivid for Spain. I talked a lot about Spain, about the hungry masses. But the local board had local goals to achieve, and we soon became sure that the Lord was nudging us out of the local situation through the enlarged vision He had given me in Europe. The feeling was nebulous, but persistent. It was a baffling experience. Radio remained foremost in my consideration of an answer for the Spanish millions.

The possibility of broadcasting to Spain seemed real enough. The need seemed so vital, but what could we do without personnel, without money? Our attempts in the States to elicit response seemed to meet with an impasse wherever we tried to share our vision. The pressure mounted inside of me as I measured the possibility of broadcasting to 30,000,000 people against the polite indifference among American Christians.

"Father, what shall we do? I just can't give it up! But I don't know what to do!"

Realizing that I could no longer be satisfied working within the boundaries of one city, I resigned my position with Youth For Christ, and announced my availability as an evangelist. It was a small step in the direction of our ultimate goal, but from a personal standpoint, the change had major proportions.

It was about this time that the Lord sent us the first of our five children, Paul David, who was born October 26, 1949. He brought great joy and happiness to our home. But we were no longer able to count on a regular salary. We had been promoted to living by faith rather than by sight. From now on the groceries and the rent would have to come directly from the Lord, rather than from the YFC office. These were testing times.

Following our first attempts to secure help for the Spanish pastors, I arrived at a revised conclusion. I began to believe that it was of utmost importance for us to move in the direction God indicated, but also that it was right for us, personally, to work diligently, putting away what money we could for the ministry that lay somewhere in the indistinct future.

We started by designing and building trailers in Scranton, Pennsylvania. Then in the Greensboro area we began building homes, some in the eight to ten thousand dollar bracket, others I custom-designed for the buyer sold for around thirty thousand. Every bit of profit we could siphon off went into a fund for "the work." Gradually the balance began to tip. As "the work" became clearer, we cut back on the building contracts, until finally we felt the proper time had come to let the construction go.

By 1951 further investigation on the continent seemed wise. This time Betty Jane went with me to Spain. Father particularly felt her passage would be money well-spent. Everyone else in the family had seen the needs of people, but for Betty Jane missions had always been second-hand. The entire amount came as gifts from Christian friends.

"It really paid off, honey," she has often said. "I'd never seen anything like it in my life, and it made me willing to go along with the sacrifices that became necessary."

Russ Reid also accompanied us. We greatly enjoyed his fellowship and ministry both in music and word.

This time when the potential of radio came up, one Spanish interpreter had said, "You ought to go over to Tangier; that's the best place for broadcasting."

I did not want to go to Tangier at all. I found myself balking at the suggestion just as I had balked when God sent me to Spain the first time. It had seemed such a waste. My whole life had been invested in the Middle East among the Arabs. Why would God choose for me a completely different people in a totally strange land?

But all He had to do was to get me into Spain—to set me down in the dark caves and crowded streets. Before I could realize what was happening my eyes were wet with tears. I understood in a very short time that the needs of the Spaniard without Christ were just as real as those of the Arab, whose life without Christ had always been such a burden on my heart.

Now the very mention of going to Tangier loomed as a threat to the ministry that had pulled me so strongly to the Spanish people. I had preached in their churches and homes. They were my people. I was warmed by their love. I enjoyed their eager response and acclaim. Why couldn't God open up broadcasting facilities right here on the mainland? Why would He want to move us to Africa? I felt somewhat like a chessman being moved across the board by a giant master mind. And I could not understand this particular move out of Spain any more than I had understood the move into Spain.

It was an older, wiser Spanish Christian, Samuel Vila, who told me of two men praying about a radio ministry for Spain. They were Peter Harayda and Ruben Lores. And he told me they lived in Tangier in North Africa!

So one morning we took the bus from Seville to Algeciras, the small Spanish town where the ferry crosses the straits to Tangier. On arriving at the North African coast we located Harayda and Lores and began sharing our mutual dream of a missionary radio station to speak to the Spaniards—hundreds of thousands of people we could never talk to in any other way.

That night at sunset, from the mountains overlooking the Straits of Gibraltar, we could see Spain. We were picnicking, outside of Tangier, on the beautiful site of a former mission school. It grieved us to think of the dedication and dreams—of someone unknown to us—that had gone into the building of this place, now lying vacant, cob-webby, and shattered. It seemed to us we might redeem it and give it new life and purpose as our visionary radio station.

Tangier was an international city, separated from Spain by only twenty-six miles of water. As we stood on Moroccan soil and looked over at Spain, we realized there was freedom here to build, whereas there might never be an opportunity in Spain. In a fragrant pine grove the six of us knelt and asked God to give us the desire of our hearts—that we might be used to bridge the straits with a clear signal of the good news of Jesus Christ for the Spanish people.

The next day we went to visit the eighty-year-old missionary, a godly old Englishman, who we learned owned the property where we had prayed. Mr. Elson had used up the years of his life in a dedication to these people. Now with a scant piece of time remaining, and a small cottage as his headquarters, he caught our vision and comprehended the intensity of our desire to reach people with the Gospel.

As we sat talking with him we recalled Torrey Johnson's earlier mandate to us, "Ask largely for things, and the most anybody can do is say no."

I decided this was one time to follow his counsel. I asked Mr. Elson to pray with me about the possibility of giving the old mission property for Gospel radio.

When we got up from our knees, the old gentleman said, "Young man, if you can give your life for missions, the least I can do is give my property."

He explained, however, that it was not a decision he could make alone for it had been promised to some relatives. After consultation with them they decided to ask fifteen thousand dollars, only a small percentage of the appraisal figure on the mission property.

Shortly after this encounter we returned home by way of Portugal. Our minds were drenched with the constant prayer that the Lord would use our tongues and our pictures and our commitment to the need to stir Christians in America to participate with us. We had no doubts now that Gospel radio was our cause, and Tangier would be the address.

Back in the States, as we tried to communicate to the churches our prayer burden for a Christian radio voice into Europe, we decided a motion picture would help tell the story. While in Spain I had taken some excellent movie shots. These formed the basis of a dramatic full color, sound film, *Banderilla,* which told Christians in North America in a very touching way the difficulty of believers in Spain. Ben Armstrong, pastor of the Community Church in Ringwood, N. J., and his wife Ruth (my sister) took a deep hearted interest in my burden and vision for Spain and helped a great deal in showing *Banderilla* in many churches across the U.S.A. and Canada.

Without any visible support Betty Jane and I and our two little children—Paul David was three, and Donna Jean only eight months—started out on an 11,000 mile deputation trip. For two and a half months I spoke and showed the film in a different church or auditorium every night. The schedule was a cruel one but it proved to be the beginning of our gaining prayer and support for Spain. It was Christmas Eve when we arrived back home.

Banderilla proved to be most helpful in arousing interest to help the Spanish pastors who had barely enough on which to live—without even considering means of expanding their outreach to the people. We did send a number of gifts but I still knew this was not God's full answer to my burden for Spain's millions.

When our only daughter, Donna Jean, was born we wondered how we would get her out of the hospital. "You can't take the baby home until you pay the bill," the ominous word had filtered down. We thought maybe some close friend or relative would be the answer. But here was an important lesson: we began to learn that things rarely come from where we expect—but when and where God wills. This time was no exception. God provided.

The same day that Donna was born—February 11, 1952—Trans World Radio got its official start, founded under the name, "International Evangelism." From the very beginning in our attempt to tackle the Spanish dilemma, criticism flowed freely around us. Much of it stemmed from our not being able to define our goals. We believed something needed to be done that was not being done, but we did not fully know what direction we should go. The thought of radio never left us, and in the back corners of our minds we continually wondered what God would open.

For both of us these were adventurous, demanding months of learning and growing. Many times we were tempted to give up. It was such a struggle. For a while, every day was almost more than we could stand. There were periods when I seemed to be operating on brute force—just constantly pushing myself to go out and tell the story, to show the film, to plead with the Lord to lay the burden on other people's hearts.

It takes courage and confidence to walk into the unknown. But often, just at the point where we felt strong and sure, we would be bulldozed by an avalanche of criticism.

"You're raising money for a station that isn't even in existence."

"You don't have an important enough board of directors."

"You don't know what direction you're going yet."

"You ought to join an existing missionary group."

"There are plenty of radio stations already in operation. Why start another one?"

All my life I've wanted to fight back. It's been a struggle time and time again. But I gradually learned that fighting back takes strength and time. It can kill the heart of a dream. We began to discover that the Lord was able to fill our hearts with love for other Christians even when they were throwing obstacle after obstacle directly into our path of progress. When criticism threatens our advance, Betty Jane and I have learned to help each other to pray that the Lord will direct and use the criticizer in the special work God has for him. How we as Christians need to pray for each other out of a heart of love—not criticism!

And we were so sure that our vision was rooted in Christ. We would not turn back. We were reassured at the point of each discouragement that this was our peculiar task. And we were not in it alone.

CHAPTER VII
BACK TO THE PINE GROVE

"It matters not how much we put into the cause of Christ," I had often observed, "but how much we hold back." It seemed as we worked our way into 1953 that God was asking me to test the words I had so easily spoken.

The day came when it became apparent that I should return to Tangier to lay the groundwork for the station. We had nothing available to finance the trip. So we sold our home and our car, and I took the money for further investigation of the radio potential in Morocco. Betty Jane and the children—Paul David nearly four, Donna Jean nearly two, and the new baby James Philip—moved into a small apartment.

My journey from the States this time took me straight to Tangier. I knew that it would take time to get the necessary permit from the government so that we could begin building the station. I was prepared to have my patience tried, for government wheels turn slowly in any land.

Upon my arrival in the port city, I started the routine that I believed would eventually produce the necessary papers for our permission to build transmitters and antennas. Negotiations were going well, and I was greatly encouraged. Then an amazing thing happened.

One morning as I was walking through the noisy streets of Tangier, an American stopped me.

"Good morning, Mr. Freed. My name is Southworth. I understand you're trying to build a radio station."

I recognized him as the man who had a radio permit and his own station in the international zone of Tangier. I wondered what he was thinking.

"I have a simple proposition," he continued. "I'd like to suggest that your station be put up under my permit."

My first reaction was negative, "No, I'm not interested in that."

"You may save a year or more in time."

"It's very kind of you to offer, Mr. Southworth, but we're doing very well, really."

"And you'll probably save some money, too."

Maybe it was pride that made me resent an outsider who wanted to barge into my dream. I had a great desire to build this dream myself—into an efficient powerful radio station. I was not interested in having someone else take it off my hands. It was mine, and I felt a surge of possessiveness about all the arrangements as I stood there in the shadow of a Moslem mosque looking at this friendly American.

That night I was restless. I was all alone in my room, and I had been reading the Bible and praying a long time.

"What are you saying to me, Lord?"

I walked around the room, picking up a newsmagazine, some papers, a picture of Betty Jane and the children. I wanted to understand why this American had been sent to me. I had to figure out why I was not eager for his help, so that the station would proceed immediately.

Finally, the drive and ambition to prove my own ability popped into sharp focus, and I knew I was trying to run the Tangier project myself. It was more gratifying for me to think of winning this battle all by myself, than it was to accept the offer of a man whom God had chosen to share in the building of His station.

By the time morning came I was ready to accept Southworth's offer as God's exact answer for us. I phoned him to say, "Yes," and we began working out the details of the arrangement. It was a marvelous solution. He would build the transmitters and antennas for us, and then lease the whole package back to us. He had the permit, the land, and the engineering crew. It would involve much less cash outlay for us—only payments over a period of time.

That day opened all kinds of possibilities to me. I saw how foolish it would be for me to try to do it all alone. I thought, when it comes to all these intricate technical details, nobody is ever going to know all the answers to everything. The most important thing, I could see then, was to get capable, technical people to do the complicated, technical jobs. People in whom I could have confidence. People who not only knew their field, but who could apply their knowledge in a pioneering setting.

I had never been a radio enthusiast. I knew a lot more about ten dozen other things than I did about radio. And it seemed rather strange that, with so many radio hams in the world, the Lord would put His finger on me for this broadcasting venture into Europe.

My mind and heart were gripped by the potential of the air waves. It seemed that radio could move across all boundaries, over the walls, through the 'curtains,' like nothing else. I thought of the world's masses of people as "one world," with the same basic needs of the heart. I knew that every individual had the right to be reached. I was sure that in God's perspective all people were beloved by Him, that with Him there were no barriers, no differences. The issue had emerged clearly. Our goal as believers comprising the Church of Jesus Christ was to reach people everywhere, without exception. Reaching them by radio was not just a theory either, for we knew that over there on the European continent there was the largest concentration of radio sets for the population anywhere in the world outside the United States.

Here was the force that could move across the mountains, into the valleys, through the hamlets and olive groves and vineyards.

Here was the force that could slip into the minds and hearts of the shopkeepers, the matadors, the dockhands, the vendors, the artisans, the farmers. Here was the signal that could penetrate the lavish mansions of the nobility, and the earthen homes of the peasants and bring life to all who would take it.

My heart was aflame with a passion to tell all those people that Jesus Christ loved them, that He died for them, that He rose again and is alive today. All they had to do was believe. BUT, they must first hear.

While I was trying to implement the idea in the States, people often warned me, "You've got to know a radio from A to Z yourself before you get into that kind of work."

That morning as Mr. Southworth talked to me, I knew those "comforters" had been wrong. Transmitters and studios and antennas were absolutely essential, but God had men ready to manage those areas if we would listen to Him. These things had to be built in the best way possible. Only certain specially trained people could do this job. But I also knew that it was just as important to plan what we would tell the listeners when all the construction was completed and we threw the switch to transmit our message of Eternal Life across the straits and into Europe.

There were many problems to be faced. From the very beginning the Lord had impressed on my mind the importance of finding someone who had actual experience in leading a staff of workers. In thinking of all the possibilities, it suddenly dawned on me that the best man I could get to manage the work in Tangier would be my own father. At that time he was teaching at the Western Canadian Bible Institute in Regina, Saskatchewan.

When I got back to America I phoned him to discuss the need for putting the best possible man in charge of the station before we could go ahead in Tangier. I was so sure that he would be the one for the job that I was baffled by his answer to my invitation, "Why Paul, just three days ago I accepted the presidency of this school."

I did not know what to say. I could not offer him anything that remotely resembled the financial security or prestige of this fine school. So far, even though the Tangier beginning was good, it was tiny. Really, all I had to offer him was the challenge of the possibility of a very large ministry, and the hope that it would become important to us all.

Father was as puzzled as I. He told me, "I don't know what I can do, Paul. But we'll pray about it."

As I hung up the phone I could imagine Mother sitting in the rocking chair with her Bible open on her lap. She was a very quiet person—always ready to fit into what would be good for her husband. "You'll know what's best, Ralph," I could almost hear her say as Father would repeat our conversation to her.

I also thought of her on her knees. Praying was not something Mother *had* to do; it was something she wanted to do. I knew she would take her pencil and add this request about the Tangier work to her prayer list. For years she had kept a record in a little notebook—a complete list of subjects for prayer, specific objectives to mention each day. I wondered how long it would be before she could come bursting with joy to Father and say, "Look, Ralph, we can cross this one off now. I've been praying for two years, or six months, or fifteen days. And now we know what God wants. Now we can cross it off."

I knew from past experience that if they believed something was right or wrong, the whole world could not move them from their position.

"Never under the shining heavens should you disobey the will of the Lord," she used to tell us children.

It was only a few days later that the telephone rang. When I heard my father's voice, the world stopped turning momentarily as I listened, "Paul, I can't get it out of my heart and mind. I know there are no funds. But Mother and I have been praying about it, and we're ready to go. All we ask is that you stand with us in prayer that God will supply the needs."

As I sat back in my chair projecting the future, I thought of what this would mean to my parents. I wondered how I'd ever had the nerve even to suggest that they start all over again. For that was what it would mean.

Father was then sixty-one, a veteran missionary who had completed a far-reaching ministry in the Middle East. God had called him and annointed him and used him. Now he was back in America, with the honor of being named president of a Bible school. It seemed exactly right, a fitting climax to his strenuous life on the mission field. But he was throwing it all out, starting all over again to help me in the brand new venture.

I was asking my parents to go back to the same place they were years before, when—walking the sidewalks of Nyack, New York—they put themselves completely on faith. They would be like young candidates just starting out.

After Father had made the decision, he explained, "Paul, we'll go out to Tangier to start this work for you. We will no longer be supported by the Christian Missionary Alliance, you know, and the normal procedure would be for us to go around to churches and raise our support. I just don't feel that the Lord wants Mother and me to do that at this point in our lives.

"Now that you know for sure that you have a director for the Tangier station, you can go out and tell your friends that the work has begun. Then as people become interested in praying, and as gifts start coming in, you can send some of it to us. Mother and I will ask no fixed amount. We'll simply spend a minimum amount for our needs, and the rest will go for radio."

When the school year ended they packed up to leave Regina, Canada, for Greensboro, N. C., where they joined us in the setting up of a workable organization. "It's kind of my pet hobby," I overheard Father chuckle.

Some six months later, in January 1954, they smiled from the deck of the former transport ship, Vulcania, as it pulled away from the pier in New York harbor. At that time there were only dormitory accommodations available, since the ship had not yet been remodeled from its troop days. I caught my breath as I waved them off to a new life in North Africa.

There were no big farewells, no delegations to see them off, no reporters shoving them for a story. But they were confident that the only place in the world for them at this time was Tangier, Morocco.

The next time I made the trip to Tangier I was on my way to a solid piece of ground that belonged to us. I could walk around it and look at it and plan on it. I could stand in the pine grove and say, "So far, it's good, Lord. Thank you."

In a sense I felt the excitement of going home after a long, long journey. To a place I could see. A place I could touch. A place I could measure . . . we had fourteen acres. And it seemed like I needed to *see* the hills, and *smell* the fresh salt breeze, and feel the

Transmitter building of "The Voice of Tangier"

pine needles prick my hands before I could realize that the long dream was over. The action had begun.

The beautiful property overlooking the Straits of Gibraltar where we had met at sunset to pray a number of months before would be ideal for studio and residences, but we had no money to buy it. One day while riding through the Pennsylvania countryside with a friend of ours, Clarence Staats, we mentioned casually the property in Tangier. Turning around to Betty Jane, Mr. Staats startled her with two direct questions.

"Does Paul know what he's talking about?" he began.

After she gave him proof of my sound judgment, he asked, "Why don't you do something about it?"

Betty Jane let out a startled, almost wounded, cry, "But Mr. Staats, it takes fifteen thousand dollars!"

After discussing the purchase further with us, Mr. Staats astonished us by saying, "I don't see why we can't arrange that for you."

The whole amount, given shortly thereafter by Mr. Staats, was mailed immediately to Father in Tangier, and he completed the transaction with Mr. Elson and gained title to the land for our station headquarters. We were confident that Tangier was an ideal location for the radio station. Statistics proved it a technically favorable point from which to broadcast into all of Europe. Voice of America had a tremendous installation just a few miles away from where our transmitting set-up was going in, and they were being heard near and far.

Meanwhile construction in Tangier had begun. We had had to choose between the simplest, and the next most simple, antenna system. If there had been more money available, we could have achieved more. The engineers with Mr. Southworth started us out with a little war surplus transmitter—2500 watts. They added a couple very simple antennas. Our budget for the first year was $10,000—less than one-hundredth of what it was to become after ten years of broadcasting.

The interest, by Europeans, in Christian broadcasting in Europe was almost non-existent when we first started in 1954. One of the reasons for the indifference among evangelicals was that apart from Monaco and Luxembourg, none of the European countries had outlets for private broadcasting initiatives. Broadcasting companies were either public, or run on a supervisory system, which set up boards consisting of bureaucratic nominees in proportion to the strength of the government parties. These companies were, because their being public institutions, bound to be pluralistic in every aspect of their programming, including religious broadcasting. Thus not only evangelical, Bible-believing Christians, but also people of very different theological backgrounds had access to the broadcast media: Listeners would be confronted, not only with a clear Gospel message, but also with liberal, unbiblical material. The concept that an evangelical pastor or Christian broadcaster could have a regular program on an evangelical station situated in Europe seemed quite impossible.

At the beginning, when my desire to awaken and develop interest was so fresh and unclouded, I found the situation as bad as knocking my head against a stone wall. The finest of Christian leaders said, "Radio just isn't our line. We understand they do that in America, but it's just not our way." Of course, they did not have the possibilities of making it their way as we have had in the States. Gaining the confidence and interest and support of European Christians was a slow, painstaking process.

In the meantime, our working, or leasing, arrangement with Mr. Southworth's Radio International there in Tangier saddled us with certain fixed obligations each month. We did not progress as smoothly as we would have liked. Funds came in very slowly. Father did not have money to buy even an old, used car. He and Mother had to wait for the bus to go to market, then teeter precariously in the crowd. Father watched every dime over there. They were out there with nothing. Back home I was hitchhiking around the United States with virtually nothing. Those were indeed difficult days.

Gradually the situation tightened. Money was just not coming in. Rent began to pile up. Father was adamant against getting into debt. Paying his bills was an integral part of his Christian testimony. All of us wanted to be a correct witness in our lives and our business dealings, as well as in the message we planned to broadcast. Bills continued to come, and there was no way to pay them.

The pressure became so critical that Father took things in his own hands. A cable reached me one morning in Greensboro, just three months after Mother and Father had sailed into Tangier, "Paul, if we don't get some real encouragement, some real help this week, I've made arrangements to give up the broadcasting business and come back."

I was heartbroken.

CHAPTER VIII
THE VOICE OF TANGIER

Some of the stories that seem stranger than fiction are just that because God moves in and superimposes His pattern on our lives. I have found so often that God will lead a Christian almost to the breaking point, or up to a final crisis, and then He takes over. Oftentimes in the history of our radio work it seemed like an impossible situation was building up, then suddenly right before me was the answer. I believe this sequence is not by accident; I believe this is exactly the way God's sovereign will works. I believe it is important in our everyday needs to do what we can with the ability He has given us. Then when we come to the end of ourselves, God steps in.

It was Saturday—the end of that week Father referred to in the cable. My heart was heavy, my mind numb. I had prayed almost constantly that God would do something to allow "The Voice of Tangier" to become a reality. Toward evening the telephone rang. It was Dr. Charles Stevens, pastor of the Salem Baptist Church in Winston-Salem, N. C. He was about twenty-eight miles away and heading in our direction.

"Paul, I'm coming through your city, and I wonder if you'd have time to meet me for a few minutes. I'm taking a Pullman train up north to start a Bible conference on Sunday."

I met him at the station and listened to him talk about the meetings he was to hold, about how their school, Piedmont Bible College, was coming, about how much the Lord meant to him. I was poor company with little to contribute to the conversation. The darkness—as we stepped out on the station platform—was a welcome cover for my dismal mood.

Suddenly I became aware of something Dr. Stevens was saying to me, "I wasn't going to tell you this, Paul, until I came back. But somehow I feel I'd better tell you right now before I go."

Dr. Stevens knew of the radio work we were starting in North Africa. He knew Mother and Father. But he certainly could know nothing of the financial crisis we were facing.

"I've been praying much about your mother and father. They've come to my heart and mind time and time again during the past week. I've decided to mention them again to my church as soon as I get back from this week of meetings. I expect Salem Baptist will want to take on virtually the full support of your parents."

I was looking down at a patch of ice on the railroad ties as he spoke. I scarcely dared raise my head as he continued.

"I thought I would wait till I had it confirmed with my church board, but I've already touched on it with them, and they've expressed themselves as being in favor of helping. We've not taken official action yet. God seemed to bring it to my heart, and the board was pleased with the idea. I just thought I'd mention it to you tonight rather than wait a week to tell you officially about it."

I reached inside my coat and took out the many-times folded and unfolded cable from my father, and handed it to Dr. Stevens. "You'll never know what this means to me!" was all I could say.

He leaned over to put his arm around my shoulder and read the cable as the train roared into the station. With a look of utter amazement he shook his head and said, "The Lord does marvelous things for us!"

If this man of God had waited a week to tell me his decision, it would have been too late. My father would have been on his way home.

Here was a friend whom God brought to stand with us when circumstances were closing in. One person after another—real friends—God had raised up along the way to share with us not only when things are bright, but also when they are pitch black.

* * * * *

One of the evangelical centers on the European continent is Beatenberg, Switzerland. It was from there that I had first gone into Spain, six years earlier following the Youth For Christ conference. It was there we were first to meet Hermann Schulte. Then later on, God led us to the men who were to be the key in the French branch and the Yugoslavian, the Rumanian, and others, right there in the same spot. Beatenberg is a small village tucked away in the Swiss Alps, about two thousand feet above Interlaken, an international resort. All year round, Bibelheim, a good European Bible school with its president, Dr. Wasserzug, trains students for ministries among German-speaking people around the world. During the summer it is a Christian conference center—the largest on the continent, open ten weeks long, with a large number of European evangelicals attending. It was logical that sooner or later Christians, vitally interested in sending out the good news of Jesus Christ by radio, would come through this little village, from a variety of European nations.

We were particularly impressed that Germany would be an important place to begin broadcasting as soon as possible. We had prayed regularly that God would lead us to the right people, not only those who would be able to stand with us financially, but those who would be uncompromising in their stand for the message of the Gospel.

Long before most others paid attention, there was one man in Germany who had already developed a keen interest in Gospel radio, so much so that he and some friends had purchased fringe time on Radio Luxembourg. It was a very bad time actually. But it was enough of a sample to sell Hermann Schulte on using radio to reach millions of people with God's Word.

Just as soon as he heard about "The Voice of Tangier"

conference, he got in touch with my father in Beatenberg. It was wonderful to see how the Lord had impressed on him the need of really helping. Hermann Schulte rallied to our burden and vision at a time when we felt that everything that needed to be accomplished added up to more than we ourselves could humanly do. In a marvelous way he brought together many outstanding Christian leaders and businessmen in Germany around the core theme of witness by radio.

From our first meeting with Hermann Schulte we were impressed that here was a man who was well-acquainted with the Lord. It seemed apparent from the start that this man would know how to help us lift the burden. We knew from our earliest conversations that he would not say, "Well, now, you just come on over and help us. We'd sure be glad to have you do a real nice series of broadcasts for our people."

Here was a man who—under God—would say, "I'm really going to take this burden and lift it with you."

I remember the tremendous comfort of suddenly realizing that right there in one of our most important target areas of Europe there were Christians concerned about helping their own people. The presence of an indigenous interest gave us a head start toward the success of our project—much more than our outside enthusiasm pouring into an unready audience could ever do.

It was at this point that I began to realize God was going to do more than just open doors. He was going to give us men who would stand in the gap with us, men who would know how to help us lift the burden. The greatest encouragement came when we understood that God had his men scattered throughout Europe—men whom He would touch as He wanted them—people totally committed to Him. All through the work I can look back and see men working here, there, and yonder. There were not a great number in any place. But dedicated to the Gospel witness among their own countrymen, these key men gathered about themselves others who learned how to come alive to the radio work.

Ruben Lores, one of those who shared in that early prayer

meeting overlooking the straits, took on the Spanish-speaking programs right away. In addition to his usual work as pastor of the local Spanish congregation in Tangier, he became a part-time radio staff member just as we were ready to begin our broadcasting schedule in February 1954. When his plans changed, taking him back to his native Cuba, we realized we were faced with finding a replacement for the very core of our work.

My father was scheduled to make his first trip to the continent since our operation had begun, and he left the station with the names of several missionaries in Spain and elsewhere who might have suggestions for us.

Arriving in Beatenberg he saw the Lord's plan begin to unfold most unexpectedly. Father tells how God directed in a wonderful way:

"I was talking with a prominent businessman and asked him to join me in prayer for a Spanish-speaking helper for 'The Voice of Tangier.'

"The next day he said he thought he knew the man who could help with the Spanish work. He had become acquainted with a young couple, the Valbuenas, graduates from the Bible School in Lausanne, Switzerland, near his home. He knew they had come to school from their home in Barcelona. I was heading there anyhow to look for someone, since the largest group of evangelicals in Spain are centered in Barcelona. It was certainly a lead worth checking out.

"When I inquired about Sr. Valbuena in Barcelona I learned he was in Canada for three months, teaching Bible in Quebec. My first reaction was, 'Well, that's that!' After looking around a while I didn't find anyone else who seemed qualified.

"My train was scheduled to leave the city at 1 P.M. The morning of departure I was strongly impressed that I should meet his wife. In just a short visit I was favorably impressed with Maria Valbuena, and I told her of my reason for being in Barcelona. As I left her she promised me, 'I'm going to write to Miguel in Canada, and let him know what you need.'

"About ten days later a letter came to us from Miguel Valbuena in Canada: 'I've been praying very much about my future ministry. I'm here in Quebec only on a visit. The Lord has been impressing me that I should not do personal work in Spain, but that He wants me in some wider ministry. I have had no idea where it would be. When your letter arrived, I felt immediately that "The Voice of Tangier" was my answer.' "

Early in 1955, Miguel and Maria Valbuena joined us in Tangier. Not only did he develop a large extension ministry among the Spanish-speaking people in addition to his programs, but he also did much to develop Bible courses throughout Spain. Maria worked out a varied schedule of related activities among the children of Tangier, as a follow-through for her extremely effective children's radio programs.

Following the Spanish and German beginnings, we were able to move into Yugoslavian and Rumanian broadcasts because of contacts also made in Beatenberg. Father had been invited several times to spend the entire summer speaking at the conference. One summer he got acquainted with Dr. Josef Horak, an outstanding government official in the Yugoslavian department of economics. He was also president of the Yugoslavian Baptist Union; but more important, he was a real man of God. Shortly after that I made a trip to Zagreb, Yugoslavia, where there was great interest among young and old alike to reach their people by radio. This visit was the beginning of a real heart link with the people of Yugoslavia.

In a country basically Greek Orthodox, and partially Moslem, it seemed a fruitful prospect to consider augmenting the ministry of the dozen and a half evangelical churches through the interest of this man. Dr. Horak began making recordings for us in his Serbo-Croatian language, with his older daughter singing for the broadcast. We discovered that even though the government is officially atheistic, there was quite a bit of religious liberty. Later our engineers were able to go into Yugoslavia and travel around with Dr. Horak, recording local church choirs and messages by several ministers. Eventually we supplied him with his own

TWR staff conference in Tangier on studio site, 1959

semi-professional tape recorder, and he did many of the messages right in his home. The tapes were then sent to us to be transmitted back to his own people in Yugoslavia through "The Voice of Tangier" shortwave system.

Another contact in Beatenberg opened the door to broadcasts beamed into Rumania. Mr. Hodoroaba, a Baptist preacher in Rumania, had fled the country some years before and escaped into France where he had organized Rumanian refugees into a Baptist congregation in a suburb of Paris. A natural enthusiast, he became excited about our station as soon as he heard about it: "I want to speak on your station!"

With the help of friends in Germany who supported his radio ministry he became a regular part of "The Voice of Tangier" ministry—both through his message and through the music of his church choir.

In the case of both Yugoslavian and Rumanian programs, we have found that they reach a good many listeners who formerly lived behind the Iron Curtain. Rumanian language programs are beamed not only into their country, but also to western Europe where there are many refugees. Through many letters that are sent to us, and friends who come out with reports, we receive appreciative accounts of what the broadcasts mean to them. Large groups—not just three or four or a dozen—gather together in homes to listen.

Starting small with these few language outlets, the work continued to grow until there were broadcasts into twenty-four different language groups. In 1956 the old transmitter was replaced with a 10,000 watter, and soon after that a second 10,000 watt transmitter doubled the new power. The old simple antenna system became more and more complex, as we beamed specific programs into almost every country in Europe, North Africa, the Middle East, and behind the Iron Curtain.

With the growing interest in Gospel broadcast by Christian workers in various countries of Europe came the pressing need for an adequate missionary staff to carry on the technical, administrative, and secretarial work of "The Voice of Tangier."

I found it difficult in those early days to find young people who would apply to us for missionary service. Most of them had never heard of "The Voice of Tangier," and the churches were slow in committing support to a new missionary organization. But in this also the Lord had His own wonderful way to break through this impasse.

In Tangier my parents prayed daily for missionary help. I wrote to my father that there were no applicants in sight. One day my parents received a letter from Anna Lee Erickson, who was one of the very promising students at the Canadian Bible Institute in Regina at the time my father taught there and Mother was Dean of Women.

Anna Lee's letter read something like this: "Through your

Miss Anna Lee Erickson, the first appointed North American missionary in Tangier

ministry in Regina I became increasingly burdened for the mission field. I have been turning over in my mind where among the great mission societies I should apply. Somehow it keeps coming to me that I would rather serve the Lord on the mission field with the Freeds than in any other place. Could you use me?" Having known Anna Lee well for three years, my parents replied the same day, "Accepted." I believe that this was the fastest processing of any application in the history of Trans World Radio.

In God's wonderful way this turned the tide, and soon applications began to come. In the beginning I personally helped with the raising of support. By the end of the first five years of operation our field staff in Tangier grew from two to twenty-six workers.

Tangier was a good front from which we could operate, and the need for new studios and permission to raise further the transmitting power kept us planning ahead. It seemed strange when the projected funds for Tangier did not come. We could not understand why, but almost from the beginning we were looking ahead for other locations on the continent.

CHAPTER IX
PROMOTED

In the spring of 1957, when I made a trip from the United States to Morocco, I had no reason to feel any problem. Everything was in order at the Tangier station. Many people were listening to our broadcasts going out in twenty-four languages. But almost subconsciously the Lord impressed me that I ought to be investigating alternate possibilities for a station location on the continent.

The night before I was to return to the States, Mother and Father and I were driving from downtown Tangier. We had stopped the car in front of the North African Mission Hospital to talk and to pray—as we had done so many times before—that the Lord would order our steps. Without too much thought I commented, "Maybe I'll go back to Greensboro by way of Monte Carlo."

As soon as I said it out loud I expected to hear, "Well, that's really out of the way, Son. That's not the thing to do."

But instead I heard Mother saying, "Paul boy, I think maybe you should go to Monte Carlo. I believe God is really in this."

I was surprised that Father too sensed it was God who was leading in this direction. Their full conviction concerning the Lord's guidance has always been a source of great encouragement to me. They never swayed in making a decision. When they were sure God was leading them, there were no alternatives, no debates. Through many experiences I have become firmly convinced that God does not have two directions for our lives. It is a matter of finding His way, and then moving into it.

All three of us prayed again. And the next morning—with great expectation—I switched from a New York City flight to a plane headed for Monte Carlo. Many times in the days ahead I was to look back on that midnight encounter as evidence of God's sure direction.

At the station Mr. E. Bosio, a Radio Monte Carlo executive, welcomed me. He was well aware of our work in Tangier, and commended us on a good job of broadcasting. He took me up on the top of the mountain where their transmitters were located. And as we looked out over the city I approached him about the feasibility of our moving to Monaco, and working through their franchise, of building a transmitter for full-time Christian broadcasting. We talked about the kind of directional antennas that would be necessary for reaching that part of the world. Later, in discussing the possibilities at length with several of the station officials, I found them very receptive. They were also concerned at that point that I not make their response public, but that we keep in touch and work out the details carefully together.

By summer the work in Tangier was moving smoothly enough for Mother and Father to take time for a much-deserved furlough trip back to the States. En route to America they decided to stop off in the tiny principality of Monaco. I had wondered what misgivings Mother would have when she actually saw Monte Carlo in all its glamour. I was sure her normal reaction would be, "This is just a little bit too fantastic!"

They checked into the Majestic Hotel facing the harbor. Father tells how she took it all in and then said, "Ralph, I feel so much that the Lord is in this whole thing."

It was September 1957 when they arrived at my sister Ruth's

home in Ringwood, New Jersey. Betty Jane and I were in the process of transferring both our home and the Trans World Radio headquarters from Greensboro, North Carolina, to the New York area—to make it a more convenient location for missionaries coming and going. By the time my parents arrived we were living just a short distance from Ruth and her husband, Ben Armstrong, who was still pastoring at the Community Church in Ringwood. It was wonderful for all of us to be together—Mother and Father, children and grandchildren. One of our celebrations centered about their fortieth wedding anniversary, the fourteenth of November. Father had such fun shopping for a little gift that would delight his sweetheart. We could all see. the joy in their lives together. It was obvious they were deeply in love, and they were each concerned about understanding and pleasing the other.

Father was away speaking a good bit at first, and I had several opportunities to be home with Mother—just the two of us. I remember her quiet thankfulness, her deep enjoyment of our fourth child, Stevie, who was eight months old at that time. In our garden one day she looked up at me from the lawn chair, and said so profoundly, "The Lord has made everything beautiful, Paul."

About the middle of November I had a speaking engagement at the Church of the Open Door on the West Coast. Some friends came to drive me to the airport. I was telling the family goodbye, when a strange thing happened. I was only going to be gone four or five days, but I suddenly had an intense desire to talk with my mother. I excused myself and went back to her room, and did something I had never done in quite that way before. Mother and I had always been very close, but for the first time in my life—with no apparent reason—I took about ten minutes to tell her how much I loved her, how much her influence had meant in my life. She started to cry. But I wanted her to know how much her life had been an inspiration to me, how sweet she had been, so I went on. I told her how glad I was that they were back in the States, and how much I was looking forward to having her close at hand for a whole year. I remember wiping away her tears, and kissing her goodbye. Then I hurried off to the car and the airport, and was soon across the continent at Los Angeles.

Since my parents were home for a rest, as well as to tell churches what the Lord was doing through "The Voice of Tangier," they decided it would be best to rent a place of their own for the year.

While I was gone the real estate agent showed them a small house overlooking a lake. The price was right, and it looked good. Mother was like a little girl with a new doll.

"Ralph, is it possible that the Lord would let us have this beautiful little place?"

Her eyes sparkled as they walked about fifteen minutes back to Ruth's home. She seemed a little weary, but she kept saying over and over how thankful she was for a lovely home of her own. How gracious the Lord is!

Father noticed she was walking more slowly than usual, but she only smiled and said, "I'm just tired." Over lunch they talked about the house, and how much fun it would be fixing it up. She was so appreciative of the Lord's goodness as she recounted the morning with the real estate agent to Ruth and Ben, and described the discovery of the little house on the lake—like a dream-home.

That afternoon she complained of a pain in addition to feeling sick to her stomach. Indigestion again, she explained, and went outside to walk around the house. She had had this trouble several times during the past years, but this time when she came in, the pain had become severe, and had extended into her left shoulder and arm.

Out on the Arabian border our family had waited on the Lord many times when there was neither hospital nor drugstore. We had not formed the habit of calling the doctor unless we were seriously ill. This particular afternoon in New Jersey, Mother was sure everything would be all right. But when Dr. Duff Brown heard of the pain in her chest and arm he recommended a heart specialist and said to get her to the hospital immediately.

Ben rode in the ambulance with her to the hospital in Montclair. He told me later that she still thought it was indigestion. The pain had subsided and she was not in any great discomfort. They joked together as they rode along with the red light making eerie passes in the darkness. Actually the whole family thought the doctor was just being overly cautious for her in mentioning the possibility of a heart ailment; she was in such good health.

It was about eight o'clock in the evening when the ambulance pulled into the emergency entrance at Mountainside Hospital. Ben saw her all settled for the night before he returned home. Father was up waiting for a first-hand report. But after he heard she was fairly comfortable, he decided to get a good rest, so he would be better prepared for a visit with her in the morning.

When I returned to my hotel out in California after the meeting, there was a message at the desk for me to call the operator in New Jersey. When the call went through my wife said she had something difficult to tell me, "Mother's had a heart attack, Paul. But the doctor says she's doing very nicely."

It was a severe shock to me. I had had no idea there was any problem when I had lingered over our goodbye. I thought about other times when God had really met her. One time in the Middle East He had miraculously raised her up from what looked like a deathbed. I was sure God would keep her with us as long as He wanted her here. I had thought about her passing away from us many times before. I knew she would have to go when the Lord wanted her to, but I felt so heavy-hearted as I hung up the phone. I walked out into the street onto the square. I asked that God would have His will in her life as He had for so many years. About 2:00 A.M. I went back to my room and fell asleep. It was only 4:30 A.M. when I was awakened by the shrill ring of the telephone.

Betty Jane sounded so close as she said, "Honey, are you sitting down?" Then after a pause, "Mother's just left us, Paul, to be with the Lord."

Even as the terrible blow of Betty Jane's words stunned me, I could also hear Mother's voice saying, "The Lord is running our lives, Paul. And He's doing it His own way."

Her sudden death was a surprise to the doctor too. The heart specialist had been called in immediately. Mother had slept well and eaten her breakfast. The charts that had been kept on her during the short period in the hospital indicated she was doing well. Everything that could have been done was done. But after breakfast, when Mother would normally be moving about, the nurse thought things were unusually quiet. She pushed open the door to check, and found Mother had passed away quietly. It was a second attack.

"She was a great example and inspiration to me, especially in times of trials," Father often said. "Unquestionably, and without exception, I knew her reaction would not be to look back, but to look ahead to learn what God has to teach us through our experiences. 'With Christ, which is far better' lay like a balm on my sore heart. The verse was a great comfort, and I asked God to give me the grace to know that for *her* it was far better."

Mother always thought of everybody else. She was a very unself-conscious kind of person. Her whole life could be epitomized by the word "prayer." She was always concerned with Father, and the family, and the radio work, never herself. Later we learned that just a few minutes before her death she had been telling one of the doctors about the goodness of the Lord and about the radio ministry in Tangier.

About eight o'clock the same morning (California time) I was in the plane heading east from Los Angeles to my family. During the flight the reality of what I had preached so many times in so many countries came to me. For the first time in my life I personally knew the reality of the glorious fact that there would be a day when I would see Mother again, face to face. I was one hundred per cent certain of this as I flew through the sky and reexamined the whole meaning of God's gift of salvation and eternal life through the Lord

Jesus Christ. Seeing Him and seeing Mother some day became an absolute reality and certainty in my mind and heart.

Even though I was numb from the shock of the news, at the same time I could understand some things with an unmistakable clarity. I could not think of just the physical loss. I could not dissociate God from the fact of her body ceasing to move and speak in our dimension. My mother had continuously lived with the Lord. And people who knew her sweet life recognized it as a result of her association with Him. Her moving beyond our reach was not some man's plan—it was God's plan to bring her into His presence.

The Lord helped all of us as we went through all the difficult things that everyone must face in time of death. We were not too well-acquainted in New Jersey yet, but we were desirous of getting someone who was close to us and who really loved the Lord to take the funeral services. Dr. Charles Stevens, whom God had sent to meet our need during the early financial crisis in Tangier, came to my mind first. When I phoned him in Winston-Salem, N. C., he had just returned from a series of special meetings in Florida. He was very tired, but he wanted to share in our sorrow in whatever way seemed best. I asked him if he could possibly come up to conduct the funeral service, and he said, "I would count it a privilege."

He knew both Mother and Father well. In fact, it was his church that had taken on their support in Tangier. He came six hundred miles to help us that day, and I will never be able to say how much he meant. In the few words he said to me personally, and in the service itself, the close tie that binds Christians was warmly and surely evident.

Mother has never come back in my thinking or in my dreams in any odd or strange way. Continuously in my mind and heart there has been the absolute conviction that my mother is no longer here, because she is with the Lord. I don't know how others would do it, but I have been back to the cemetery only two or three times since the day of her funeral. It is not that I deliberately shun it. I could go by any time. But Mother is not there. She is with the Lord.

On the other hand, my mother is just as living a reality now as she was when she was here. Her walk with the Lord, the glory of her everyday living with Him, are actual realities to me today. Her life continues with me; at the same time she is with the Lord, where we will join her someday. With incredible force this experience with death made me know the true reality of life, eternal life that is ours through the Lord Jesus Christ.

I did not have any of the feeling, "Now I can't live—life has lost everything." Life lost nothing for me. The very next Sunday I could speak at the church where I had an appointment, and feel it was just where she would want me to be. Mother would want us to go on telling people of the same God she knew and loved.

I remember Mother once coming to me after I had used her as an illustration in a sermon. "Paul boy, you just behave yourself now. Don't talk about me to the people. You talk about the Lord Jesus Christ."

I loved her deeply, and the love we knew has been translated since her death into a power for everyday living.

Perhaps death teaches us a lesson in the balance of Christian living—the balance between knowing that we are creatures born anew into a spiritual world, and knowing that we are human beings living a daily earthly existence. Our emphasis on eternal life and our hope in Christ must include a genuine interest in living fully where we are. Both our daily, earthly routine and the glorious reality of our citizenship in heaven are essential facts of Scripture. Mother's life among us exemplified so well that both are essential emphases of true balanced Christian living.

Knowing that her position with God was one hundred percent safe and secure in Jesus Christ, enabled her to have an abundant life in her daily schedule wherever she was. Hers was a life that reached up to the Lord, and out to others who needed Him too.

Betty Jane later confided in me that she had wondered if Mother's death might cause the whole work to slow down, or stop.

"Yet in my heart," she added with a smile, "I knew it wouldn't be that way, Paul."

CHAPTER X
NEW ENCOUNTERS

One of the things Mother had wanted for me was my doctorate. It was not that I was uninterested in getting it, rather that something else always received top priority in my planning. Now that she was gone, the memory of her desire for me provided the impetus I needed to shove this task to the top of the list. The week after her death I set the wheels turning and actually took one of the first big examinations in my Ph.D. program.

The School of Education at New York University helped me clarify my three-department thesis: international relations, mass communications, and religious education. The title was long and involved: "A Study of the Extent to which the Indicated Objectives of American-produced Religious Radio Programs Prepared for Broadcast in Europe would be Achieved According to French, German and Spanish Religious Leaders."

Many evangelicals told me that a Christian cannot go into a secular university without compromising his testimony. It is impossible to take a real stand for Christ in the avowedly scholarly halls of ivy, they said. My personal experience at NYU compels me to rush to the defense of those men under whom I worked. The conditions are there, and it is necessary for a Christian intellectual, as well as an agnostic seeker, to qualify before he can be respected as an honest student. However, if a person is actually studying logically toward a degree, if he will state his premises accurately, if he will be honest about the delimitations of his work and the study he has done, if he is willing to do a careful job of defining his terms adequately, if he has the knowledge to defend his thesis, he will have the academic respect of those in his department, regardless of his faith. Then the only thing that is asked of us is that we follow normal scientific procedure, sound documentation, and logical thought patterns.

In this university I found that I could very well start with the premise that the Bible is the Word of God. The great majority of people there do not believe it to be so; but I had a perfect right as a scholar to state this as one of my premises. The first scholarly step in a thesis is to spell out certain premises and delimitations, to define certain terms. After that has been done, then the university will expect logical procedures and conclusions from the basic premises. I found that thinking people did not criticize or belittle our work. They had no basis for judging us illogical once we had started with a clearly stated premise that there is a God, and that the Bible is His Word to men.

The two and a half years of study and research for my Ph.D. degree assisted our preparation for expansion onto the European continent. The main directives from my dissertation gave us usable information in our missionary radio programming. One significant requirement stood out above all others as I tabulated and evaluated the results of our research. The random samplings of opinion by tape, in person, through questionnaires, with panels of representative indigenous people, from listening to what was already being broadcast to nine main European centers—all of it pointed clearly to one important factor for successful communication. The broadcasts must be related to everyday experience, everyday life, everyday problems. The key to the Christian life is not necessarily the spectacular appearance of God in the burning bush, but His abiding presence in the disappointments, the struggles, and joys of the home, the office, the shop, the foundry, the sporting arena. Sound doctrine in our programs was essential as a foundation, but we wanted to be sure also to give instruction in how to live the Christian life.

During this period of working on my dissertation at New York University, I corresponded with Mr. Bosio and dropped in at the Monte Carlo station several times to keep the issue of expanding alive. At times I wondered if the whole business was not a waste of time. We were doing well in Tangier at that time. In fact, in the very midst of the discussions with Monte Carlo, we were close to making a real outlay to expand the facilities at Tangier. Now it is evident as we look back that where normally we would have pressed ahead on our expansion plans, here we felt inclined to move slowly. We were talking of getting new land and a bigger antenna system. But God slowed us down.

Suddenly Morocco became independent and the political picture began to shift rapidly. An announcement from the government made our delay in Tangier perfectly clear: all radio in the country was to be nationalized by the end of 1959. It was then April. It seemed black as midnight when the news first came to the staff in Tangier. Father read the notification from the government to the Wednesday afternoon prayer group. It was a tremendous blow, but not a single person said, "Well, guess we'll have to go back home."

We all knew that across the Straits were all those radio sets—an estimated 80,000,000 at that time. And we knew there was no full-time Gospel radio station on the continent. So we expected that God would do something. There was some real praying, and those tense days were filled with emotion and anticipation.

"Lord, what do You have for us? If You're closing this door, show us what You have for us next." The feeling that God would open another broadcasting opportunity was unanimous throughout the group.

When the announcement by the Moroccan government

reached our headquarters in Chatham, New Jersey, we felt as though the bottom had dropped out of everything. But the Lord was moving us rapidly now in another direction. Within twenty-four hours I was in flight from New York to Monte Carlo. We had no tangible assurance of anything developing there, and I would not have pushed a contract through earlier if I could have. All of us in the work felt certain in our hearts that we were just getting a good start in Gospel broadcasting, and we were strangely sure that the Lord was going to work something out in our behalf. Finding a place in Europe where we could build a transmitter for full-time Christian broadcasting had seemed the most difficult thing in the radio field. Many other Christian leaders had also found this very definitely to be the case. All the other continents had such transmitters, but Europe—with the largest concentration of radio sets outside the U. S.—had none. We had looked into many places on the continent for a new station site, but as far as I was concerned, Monte Carlo was the only real possibility.

During our early negotiations there, the need for a station was not urgent. By the time our need became urgent, Monte Carlo had made up its mind. At the very moment of our crisis, they were ready to talk specifically about contract agreements. Yes, God had been holding the expansion of "The Voice of Tangier" for a period of time because He had something greater in His overall plan. He did not want us wasting our efforts, or His money, adding on to a project which was soon to end. It was God's miraculous timing all around!

I was able to pick up transactions in Monaco immediately and move ahead with confidence and vigor. It was April 1959 when we started laying solid plans for our franchise with Radio Monte Carlo. Father and I prayed much about our arrangements with the radio board, and finally—with great deliberation—we decided we would have to offer them an advance of $50,000. We had no idea where we would get it, but we felt it would be an insult to offer them any less than that.

However, when I talked with Mr. Bosio, he asked, "Do you

want the Board of Directors to approve this agreement? You can put down anything you want, you know. But if you really want this to pass, you probably should be ready to offer advance payment covering the total cost of the installation. That would be about half a million dollars. I believe that's the only way they'll approve the agreement."

It seemed that Mr. Bosio was trying to help us understand how important it would be to make an offer that would be attractive to the Board—an offer they would have no qualms about accepting. He hinted that we would have a one-shot opportunity on a take-it-or-leave-it basis.

We knew the Board of Directors had already detailed the installation costs on the great antenna system and the 100,000 watt transmitter we would need. We did not have the exact

The TWR shortwave antenna system on Mount Agel high over Monte Carlo

figures, but Mr. Bosio had estimated they would total about a half a million dollars. We also knew the Board would not be interested in investing any of its own funds. It would all have to come from our little group. Mr. Bosio suggested that we consider breaking the total sum into six payments, with the first to come due at the time they approved the project. The other five could then be paid within a year while the transmitter and antennas were being installed.

It was one month until the projected Board meeting, and we felt we were going for the moon. Even the one-sixth figure for the down payment—$83,000—sounded fantastic!

While we were all thrilled at first at the possibility of moving our radio operation to Monte Carlo, our second reaction was different. A sort of shock wave hit me, and I honestly wondered if I had lost my mind. While we were drawing up the contract, Father and I spent hours and hours talking and praying. We had to "strike while the iron was hot," and we had no one but God to whom to turn. To have discussed it publicly or even with other individuals would have greatly jeopardized the possibilities of the contract going through. The working out of each detail and decision brought Father and me very close to each other, and to the Lord. But a half million dollars sounded almost hopeless !

Mr. Stanley Clark, a director of Barclay's Bank for the whole Middle East, had been a close friend of my parents for many years. Although he was not able to help financially with the Monte Carlo project, he was a great encouragement to us as we incorporated into the contract—on naked faith—the making of payments ten times as big as we had ever expected. Mr. Clark stood behind us one hundred per cent, giving advice, putting us in touch with the right people, even meeting with some of the officials for us. A British leader with a real Christian testimony among the Plymouth Brethren, Mr. Clark had once been named Governor of the United Nations International Conclave in Israel. He was used to receiving and entertaining such people as Emperor Haile Selassie and his Empress in his home, but he seemed equally at home with us. He continually demonstrated to us the effectiveness of a life really given to the Lord. His was a day-by-day translation from personal faith to significant action.

At the same time the authorities at Monte Carlo were requesting that the proposed agreement be kept confidential for the time being, they were also requiring this down payment of $83,000 which sounded like $83,000,000 to us!

The contract was a severe test of our intentions and our ability to fulfill future obligations. The equipment they were to install would belong entirely to Radio Monte Carlo, but they would not finance it. So the arrangement stated that we would pay the half million—the total cost of the installation in advance—which would give us leasing of the radio facility full time for ten years with an indefinite number of renewals. Our original investment would be coming back to us gradually then through leasing and operating costs.

It was a rigorous thing for us to face! A Swiss lawyer, on scrutinizing the contract, seemed outraged until we explained to him that Radio Monte Carlo was not coming to us, begging us to join them in Monaco, but that it was the other way around. This was the only radio station in all of Europe that would consider—at any price—allowing us the privilege of broadcasting the Gospel full time. That was true in August 1959 when we were drawing up the contract. It is still true today. Since we desperately wanted the opportunity to share their franchise, it was not unreasonable to expect a difficult and high price tag to be attached.

Some time earlier Mother and Father had made a trip to England to visit Keswick and some English friends. During this time Mother had become ill with bronchitis; later, when pneumonia set in, she had to enter a London hospital. It had been a trying time for Father who wondered why they should have their plans altered and their return to Tangier delayed by six weeks. One afternoon, frustrated and impatient, he said to himself, "Why not try and listen to 'The

Voice of Tangier'?" He hooked up an old radio and settled down after supper to tune in the English language broadcast. When he heard familiar music and voices he got so excited he ran out in the hall of the Missionary Rest Home and called, "Come and listen!"

About twenty people did come. Among them was a young Christian from Norway who was in Great Britain to study and perfect his use of the English language.

He became very interested in the broadcast, asking, "Do you think this could be arranged into Norway? We only have government radio in Norway. This is an exciting thought—that a broadcast like this might be heard in our country."

"I don't know why not!" Father said.

"Why don't we do it then?"

"Because we need people who can prepare programs and translate. And we need someone to help with the cost of putting them on the air."

"I think I know exactly the man who would be interested."

"All right, give me his name and address, and I'll sit down and write him."

One step led to another to put us in touch with the leading men in the active laymen's movement in Norway: Mr. Vaagen, Mr. Eikli, and Mr. Haanes and his son, Leif. Their intense interest in Gospel broadcasting gave us our answer to why the six weeks delay in London. Accommodations had been very poor—drafty and cold, but Mother had never wavered in her insistence that the Lord had a purpose in it. The story which follows reveals how this purpose became apparent.

Between the drawing up of the contract, and the meeting of the Board, there was less than a month. I was scheduled for my first trip into Russia at the same time to see first hand what could be done through Gospel broadcasts to that country. Enroute I stopped in Oslo and met the Norwegians who had been so excited the previous summer about "The Voice of Tangier."

I was invited to the home of Mr. and Mrs. Vaagen. That night a few friends, including the Haanes family, met for prayer. Mr. Haanes, owner of a large shipping company and several other successful businesses, was a wonderful Christian layman. I also learned that, before their marriage, Mrs. Haanes had been a missionary to Africa, a background which added experience to their keen interest in evangelism. Their son, Leif, was also a part of the prayer group.

Our fellowship in prayer was simple and sweet. They asked God to be with me in the Soviet Union. It was of particular importance to me that this would not be just a sightseeing trip. I have never sensed the power of God more fully or the assurance that He would fulfill His own purposes more completely than I did that night. I felt definitely led of God to let them know right then about the Monte Carlo possibility, and asked them to say nothing about it to anyone.

Here were influential, capable people who loved the Lord and put Him first in the way they lived out their lives. Within the Lutheran Church in Norway, God had been working quietly, touching a man here, a woman there. Spiritual awakening in the lives of many laymen had brought about an unusually concerned community of believers in Norway. Some 2,000 prayer houses had been established by this time for prayer and Bible study. This opening to the mind and heart of God further led them to be alert to service opportunities which could expedite the proclamation of the Gospel to others. They already were sponsoring several large foreign mission projects when they took to heart the radio burden which I shared with them. In downtown Oslo they now have a headquarters building where direction is given to all the prayer houses and missionary projects. I have never felt the presence of the Lord more closely than I did that night in Oslo as I prayed with these members of the Norwegian Laymen's Movement!

The little Norwegian prayer group, our German friend Hermann Schulte, and about five others outside of our family were the only people who knew of our great new challenge. The Monte

Carlo authorities had asked us not to publicize the negotiations and we also felt it unwise to do this, so we had laid no public groundwork for making the need known. As a matter of fact, we had to do the reverse—we had the amazing privilege of just resting in prayer during that strategic month.

About the same time, September 1959, we decided to set up an office for Trans World Radio on the continent. We asked a relatively new staff couple, Burt and Sonja Reed, to go with my father to open a European office in Beatenberg. The objectives were clear: one, we needed to terminate the base of operations in Tangier as headquarters; two, we wanted to lay the groundwork for broadcasting in Monte Carlo.

The work which my Father had been doing in Tangier was vital to the effectiveness of our broadcasts. However, the preparation of

The transmitter building on Mount Agel high over Monte Carlo

the programs, the follow-up, the coordinating of the increasing staff left little time for another extremely important facet of the overall project—the contacting of evangelical leaders in all the target areas of Europe. This was a dream that had had little implementation thus far.

Two weeks after his arrival with the Reeds in Beatenberg, Father went to Monaco for the meeting with the Radio Monte Carlo Board. The impossible had happened! The sum of $83,000 was there waiting! Following the prayertime in Oslo, the Haanes family had decided that God wanted them to make this first step possible themselves. They dipped deeply into their bank account and came up with the miracle check for Trans World Radio. Leif Haanes, the son, came down from Norway to convey the gift and to be present at the signing of the contract.

Stanley Clark also came to the station for the transaction. A man unique in his vision and drive, he had been amazed at the step of faith we were taking in our move to Monte Carlo. But Mr. Clark was used to stepping out boldly on faith to implement his own plans with action, so he was ready to back us completely at the Board meeting.

By this time I had returned to Chatham from the Russian survey trip, and was awaiting word from Father by telephone.

The morning the Radio Monte Carlo Board met, my father, Mr. Clark, and Leif Haanes gathered together for prayer. Later they went up on the mountain to look over the facilities. The station had been built during the Nazi regime as a propaganda station. It was a great, beautiful, massive, stone structure—just about completed, but without any equipment installed at war's end when the Germans went back to their own country. It literally made chills run up and down my spine when I thought about the Gospel going forth every day from the same structure Adolph Hitler had designed to spread Nazi propaganda.

While the three of them were up about 2500 feet above the city looking at transmitting facilities, Mr. Bosio phoned my father there.

"Good news for you! I won't tell you officially, because Mr. Solamito, our president, should tell you himself. But I'm sure you can guess. He wants to see you right away."

The next morning the transaction actually took place and Leif Haanes—with my father by his side—turned over the $83,000 check to be deposited to the Radio Monte Carlo account.

I was in my study at home when the phone call came. I felt my heart swell inside of me. I held my breath as if I were about to hear the voice of God. Then Father came on, "Paul, God has done it!"

CHAPTER XI
MIRACLES IN MONACO

By this time we had discovered that the question should never have to be: How much does it cost? But rather: Is it the will of God?

In Tangier we felt we were in the place God had chosen, and He supplied our needs from the time we started with an old used 2500 watt transmitter right on through the final stage when we were operating with two 10,000 watt transmitters. Whatever our need, the provision was always sufficient. Now in the Monte Carlo advance we were experiencing His same careful attention to our every need.

Most definitions of the will of God have a core of truth in them. Some say His direction can be determined through circumstances, some through the counsel of godly people, some through the instruction of Scripture, and others through the opportunities that present themselves obviously to us.

All these are sound and good, but they must become a pattern of daily Christian living. I believe that all of these are guidelines in selecting a course of action. But only as we *want* to choose His counsel—down to the smallest decision of each day—will we find confidence in moving ahead as He wants us to move, when a major decision confronts us. If today we are open to His direction—no matter what we are doing, then tomorrow will develop according to His will for us. If today we are in His will, then tomorrow we will be there too.

Is it not then a little presumptuous to say: "I *happened* to do this?" or "I *happened* to meet so and so?" or "By *chance* we ended up doing thus and so?" I believe that when lives are ordained of God, things do not just happen or come about by chance. If we carefully meet the Lord in our secret hearts, asking Him to search us and direct us, then it seems to me that what comes to pass—the opportunities that come before us—should be seriously considered as part of God's will. If you are in a particular spot and you run into a certain person, if you even walk to the store or take a trip, and all of these things are done with your heart open to the Lord, must you not then assume that He is directing you in the path of His will?

Of course, as long as we have the limitations of this earthbound existence, this will not be foolproof because Satan is active too; I know. But I say these things to point up the fact that some of the circumstances that occurred during our search across the continent for a place to broadcast did not *just happen*. Like the sudden desire I had to visit Monte Carlo the night Mother and Father and I were praying together in Tangier. I believe that God led me that way. When opportunities like this come before us, we seriously examine them: "Maybe this is God's direction." When doors tend to swing open or closed, the foolproof way is to go back to His Word with prayer to be sure.

Too often today we will close our eyes to opportunities He is giving us, particularly if the opportunity looks strange or difficult or unconventional. It is very important for Christians who want to do business with God to move ahead when He gives a directive.

The tremendous challenge in missions before us is the need to link arms—hands and hearts together—to work at the job. We must live in a much bigger way, with much greater vision, realizing the potential is unlimited when we commit our all to the Lord Jesus Christ. I believe with all my heart that we are lagging behind. We talk about the "jet age," about the miracles of modern science, about the tremendous strides in all areas of learning, but the greatest way for Christians to move ahead is through total commitment to Jesus Christ, absolute abandon to His use of our energies.

Today I am looking for a complete new era in Christian missions. As a comparatively young man, I would not presume to tell others what is right or wrong. I see godly men, experienced in the ways of God and of men, great Christian leaders, and I cannot presume to tell any of them what they should or should not do. But I do believe it is high time in foreign missions, and in all kinds of Christian work, that we stop living in the Dark Ages. We are still living in the past century with many of our methods.

The message never changes from one century to another. That hard plodding, going down into the village, talking face to face with people, establishing the local church, must never stop. But we do need to catch a vision that we are losing ground—every day, every week, every month, every year. Christian broadcasting is not the only answer. It is only a small part of the total outreach—radio, literature, audio-visuals, missionary aviation, translation, programmed instruction are all new ways in which we can move out in geometric proportions. We need a continually renewed vision of ways to reach others. Compared to the rest of the world's progress, Christendom is dragging at a snail's pace. I must make it very clear, though, that winning people to Christ will require both methods, the personal touch and the mass media.

Dr. V. Raymond Edman, beloved former president of Wheaton College, used to tell us in his chapel talks, "Never doubt in the dark what God has told you in the daylight." Sometimes the voice may be quiet, almost gone, and we will start to wonder.

Once God has made something clear to us, it is important that we move solidly ahead on it, not allowing little quirks and kinks along the way to deter us or make us jump off the track one way or another. Our entire life is in His keeping power. Yes, mountain top and deep valley experiences are common to most Christians. But perhaps God looks at it more like this: "I flung the stars into place; I hold the earth in the palm of my hand; why won't little man let me guide him too?" It is a real mistake, a real detour, to think one day that the life of faith is working marvelously, and the next day to think it is an awful failure.

True, there have been varying circumstances in our course of progress, and there probably always will be, but God does not change. And circumstances will not change Him. That is why I am sure that the most important thing in the Christian life is to depend on Him—no matter how large or small the question, or the decision, or the crisis. That is the key to a consistent life, a consistent ministry.

The shimmering lights of Monte Carlo at night

It was a miracle of God that TWR was able to get into Europe. Until comparatively recently, Europe had very little in the way of Gospel broadcasting. The public broadcasting systems in the various countries did not allow for individuals or private groups to purchase airing time, although they did allot a certain amount of broadcasting time to the established Churches, free of charge. Nor did the laws of the various countries permit the setting up of privately-owned stations. A Gospel minister in any country in Europe would shake his head and say, "We hear in America that preachers have radio programs, but we don't have anything like that here."

This was the picture into which God inserted Trans World Radio. People just could not believe it. When we were talking with officials at Monte Carlo, they asked us, "What will you broadcast?"

"Messages from the Bible . . . good music . . ." I answered.

"That will be all right," they said to my amazement.

"What language can we use?"

"Any language you want."

My father's move to Beatenberg, Switzerland, became a marvelous opportunity for him to meet Christian leaders from all over Europe, indigenous churchmen with whom he could share the enormous possibilities of magnifying the Gospel witness in their own countries by means of radio. As mentioned earlier, our entire German, French, Yugoslav, and Rumanian branches grew out of fruitful contacts that Father was able to make during that relatively brief period we maintained an office in that great Bible conference center.

I believe that God works through individuals—men and women given over to Him. I am convinced that He lays the burden to help on individual hearts, at a particular time, for a particular reason. During the period in Beatenberg, God was touching men here and there, raising them up to gather others about them. This is the way the Trans World Radio idea came alive among evangelical leaders in Europe and began to move. The root of every one of our expansions can be traced back to an individual whom the Lord introduced to us.

Always it is God opening the door, raising up the man, bringing in the money. Sometimes it is not when we do something, but when we do *not* do certain things that the next step opens up. We have tried to be ready to move ahead and do the job at hand, but we also have learned to expect that as we wait, we will see Him move. I have felt so many times like Moses, whose arms were held up by Aaron and Hur. The men God has touched in the various countries really do hold us up. And they have continued to stand with us "through thick and thin."

Aside from the changed lives that result regularly from the broadcasts, the greatest blessing to me of the entire work is the evidence of men rising to meet the spiritual needs of their own countrymen. Their response cannot depend on what they will get back personally, for every time it means a sacrifice on their part. They are men to whom Jesus Christ is not only real, but Lord. So many times when I would go out and select somebody for a job, I would be wrong; but God always had the right man for us in His time.

The way the work in Monte Carlo developed was amazing—one miracle after another. In the first place the beautiful Cote d'Azur—playground of princes, resort area famous for gambling—hardly seemed a likely center for a Gospel ministry. The whole thing seemed so far out, so impossible. We saw no source of income as we began talking with the Radio Monte Carlo executives. We looked about us at the permanent diadem of bougainvillaeas, carnations, trees, and flowering shrubs, at the famous casino, and marveled that we should be here at all. The only reason we went ahead was simply that we believed this was something God wanted done. We expected therefore that He would run it.

We saw the first evidence of this in the miracle check for

$83,000, given for the down payment by our Norwegian friends. But there were five more payments of approximately $83,000 each to be paid in less than a year. The very thought of these immense payments was staggering.

The second payment of $83,000 seemed even more impossible than the initial payment. We figured we would have to have the cash in our New Jersey office by noon on a certain day in order to get it to the Monte Carlo bank by noon of the next day when it was due. This was the deadline the bankers had given me in order to effect our transaction in time. We had been praying much about it; many interested friends had sent in gifts. But as we checked the total amount on the morning of the last day, we found we were $13,000 short of the stipulated amount due. Our entire staff met in the front office in the Chatham, New Jersey, headquarters. All of us stood around, reviewing the marvel of the $70,000 that had come in. Even before we opened the morning's mail, we asked God to do something—we laid our need very specifically before Him. It was a real faith-believing prayer meeting. We, as Christians, need to remember that God is not something out yonder, or something imaginary. We can bring real situations to Him. He is very much a person—One who really cares.

We prayed and then the secretary opened the mail. Suddenly she let out a cry.

"Look what's here!"

In a plain envelope with just an ordinary stamp, she had found a check for $5,000! After that we all fully believed that something more would happen.

The morning ticked away. The mail had been all opened and sorted, but there were no more gifts. It was 11:30, and I said to the workers around me, "Well, this is it. I'll have to leave for the bank or I won't make it."

There was a heavy penalty for missing this payment—something like an additional sum of ten per cent of the payment. Even more important, I thought about the clause that had been written into the contract, that at any time a payment is *not* made on schedule, Monte Carlo will have the right to drop the entire transaction.

I was $8,000 short as I got into my car and started for the bank. On the way I saw one of our workers walking along the street. When he waved, I pulled over to the curb.

"Here's a letter I just picked up at the Post Office," he said. "There wasn't anything else."

I stuck it in my pocket and drove on to the bank. After I parked the car I slit it open. I could hardly believe what I saw—another check for $5,000.

The president and two other bank officials acquainted with our TWR transaction met me as I walked in. "How are things coming along?"

"Quite well," I said, flush with the surprise and size of the two checks, and wondering what might happen next.

"That's good," and the president smiled wryly, "but very unfortunately you won't be able to handle this transaction, because you're still $13,000 short."

"Oh, no sir, we're not," I hurried to explain. "We're only $3,000 short. I have two checks here with me that just came in this morning—for five thousand apiece."

The men gasped. "This is amazing!" They could hardly believe it. They were almost as excited as I was. Here we were this close. All of them were trying to think of some way to make up the comparatively small amount that was still necessary.

"We just don't know what to do! To be just this short, and still not make it kind of surprises us."

Not knowing what to say, I shrugged my shoulders and commented, "Well, I'm sure something will happen."

By this time we were in the president's office, and the phone rang. The president almost dropped the telephone. Then he placed it back on the cradle and looked at me in disbelief, "How in the world can this happen?"

"Well, who was it?" I managed to stammer.

"Western Union, Dr. Freed. It was a telegram that has just come in, wiring funds to the account of Trans World Radio here at the Chatham Trust Company—in the amount of $3,000."

He dropped his voice at the end of the sentence, so that I almost imagined the amount rather than hearing it. Then he continued, as he sat up in his chair, and looked directly at the rest of us.

"I sure wish I knew who sent it!"

I quietly said to myself, "Well, I know who sent it. God sent it!"

"Who did you say?" he leaned over the desk toward me.

Still shaking my head, I repeated, "God sent it."

It still did not make sense to him. "I didn't quite hear you. What was the man's name?"

This time I turned to him, and repeated slowly and deliberately, "Almighty God sent it."

Now it was the banker who shook his head, and said almost inaudibly, "You know, I believe you're right."

By this time the tremendous miracle had begun to sink into my mind. I stood up and exclaimed, "Gentlemen, I know I'm right."

There were tears in his eyes as he shook off the disbelief, muttering, "This is amazing. This is absolutely amazing."

It *was* amazing. When we had talked about $83,000, it could have been $83,000,000 or $40,000 or $117,000. We had nothing. But the amount was $83,000. And here was precisely that amount to cover the payment. To the exact dollar!

By now we were free to let people know of the need in every way possible. While Father's personal financial policy required trusting the Lord without talking to anyone, we both believe that in the work of the Lord people want to know what is going on, they want to be informed of the advances, they want to share in the needs.

Modern-day missions seem to be spurting out ahead to challenge churches to give much more than they ever have before. Young people particularly are thrilled by the contemporary media. We believe God is demanding that we move into modern means as they become perfected—not to replace all the traditional lines of evangelism, but to add to them. We need to be ready to move out in real vision as God opens doors. We Christians must not be afraid of newness, the strangeness of moving into unfamiliar areas. One church, already giving $50,000 annually to missions, was so stirred by the presentation of what can be accomplished by radio that in one weekend they pledged $8,000.00 more. We do not plead or beg, but we do believe others should have the opportunity of standing with us. And as the Monte Carlo project proceeded, help kept coming to us from all directions.

A number of well-known American and Western European broadcasters were interested, and contributed varying amounts to share in the cost of broadcasting with us. "Back to the Bible," "Hour of Decision," "Old Fashioned Revival Hour," "Light and Life Hour," "Temple Time," and many other established programs advanced payments in lump sums so as to help us meet the heavy obligations during the year of preparation before we actually went on the air. Many of them had launched out by faith themselves in earlier days of radio.

Funds came in many ways—almost as much from Europe as from America. People made gifts, and churches made gifts. And then there were loans, many of which turned into gifts later on. We felt a great ground swell of blessing. The sincerity of the plan, the belief in Europe's great need for the Gospel gripped men and women everywhere. We just told them what was on our hearts, and they caught the vision and stepped forward to stand with us.

The German brethren were particularly ready to take a vital part in the financing of radio that would penetrate behind the Iron Curtain. Father had met Hermann Schulte in Switzerland the month before the proposed contract with Monte Carlo was to be approved. They talked about it, then prayed together—he and his wife, and Father. He asked us to let him know by telegraph as soon as the contract was signed, and he would immediately go to work to get support for us. He thought he would be able to interest evangelical Christians—businessmen and church leaders in Germany. It sounded wonderful and we had a lot of confidence in him based on his successful support of the Tangier work. But I could not help wondering how much he would be able to fulfill, how much he could do. There was no precedent for people in Europe contributing to the support of a transmitter broadcasting the Gospel full-time, because there was no other in existence there. Hermann Schulte and the men he contacted pledged much support on a regular basis. When they realized the huge step they had taken, there were some anxious days. In fact, every two months as the payments came due, they had a time of anxiety and prayer. But Schulte was God's man in Germany, and the people began to say, "This is for us! This will help reach more of our people. We need to get behind this and help them." Before the broadcasting facilities were fully completed, the German people unbelievably had raised over a quarter of a million dollars for the new Gospel broadcasts.

Missionary-mindedness seems to go in cycles. In Germany the Christians are very eager to move ahead and do something to reach as many of their countrymen as possible. The hideousness of the Nazi regime and the wholesale slaughter of the Jews have made the life with God particularly imperative to them. Once they meet the Savior they are anxious to do all they can to make Jesus Christ known to others.

I marvel as I look back on those unusual months. Each one of the six payments came about through a real miracle. One payment, for example, required an even larger sum than the others. As the funds came in for this third payment of $93,000 we had been sending them along to Barclay's Bank to apply against our account, rather than waiting for a lump sum to collect.

Everything possible had been done. Many personal sacrifices had been made. Great sums of money had come in from Europe—much of it from West Germany in German marks. But when the tally was made, the afternoon before the payment was due, we were short $1500. It was so very amazingly close! Yet, we could see nothing more to do.

The next morning down at Barclay's Bank, the man in charge of our account said, "No other funds have come in. But if you don't mind, I'd like to take a few minutes to refigure it."

He returned with a mysterious smile, "You made it!"

"What do you mean, we made it?" I asked.

"You'll never believe it, but the value of the German mark has jumped in value since we figured the total yesterday—which adds exactly $1500 to your balance!" He pointed to the figures on his sheet. "That brings your account up to $93,000!"

To me this was another miracle. As I leaned forward to take it all in I wondered, why do we find it so incredible every time something like this happens? I thought back to my childhood and the little two-room cottage at Nyack overflowing with food. I cannot understand God's miracles. Even with such startling evidence woven through my experience I have to admit that my

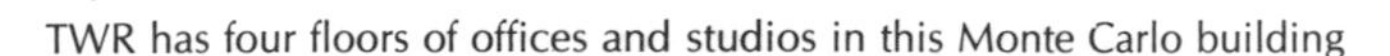

TWR has four floors of offices and studios in this Monte Carlo building

faith has been weak. Problems and trials come and I forget that we have a God who hears us and arranges His best for us. But to know God is to remember His past mercies and to know He can do abundantly above all that we ask, or even think. After all, God has been running this business since the day He headed me so unwillingly into Spain back in 1948. And He's been specializing in miracles since the world began.

CHAPTER XII
READY TO ROLL IN MONTE CARLO

During the year of construction and preparation in Monte Carlo, Betty Jane and I decided it would be best for all of us to move to Europe. Some of our friends felt obligated to tell us what a terrible expense we were going to; but I knew it was just the opposite. I could not have afforded to go at all for that long if I could not have taken my family with me. Their presence with me allowed freer concentration on the job at hand. My wife was able to be with me in love and understanding and in prayer. The children watched each step of the building. And the whole family toured several of the "target countries" with me—all six of us in the little Volkswagen.

One of the most meaningful things out of my childhood was my parents' willingness to involve my sister and me in all levels of their lives. Their pattern is being repeated as much as possible in our home. I want my children to remember not only reading the Bible and family prayer, but playing ball, fishing, swimming, traveling, working, walking—doing all kinds of things together. We have been very open with the family.

While it sounds as though I travel a lot, and am responsible for a great number of meetings, I consciously plan my schedule to avoid any extended time away from home. Sometimes it is hard for others to understand how important the children are to me. For instance, when a church asks me to come for a continuous series of meetings, I usually answer, "I could come to your area for a few nights, but then I'll need to go back home." They know, of course, that it costs less for me to come and stay through the entire series. But I have to answer that reasoning something like this, "You can't buy the value of my children's lives!"

If someone calls suddenly or comes in from Los Angeles when I am having dinner at home, I must act in accordance with the fact that I regard my appointment with the family as having the same importance as any business engagement.

I believe that it is the duty and rare privilege of a Christian father to take the time and the effort to know and understand his own children. From my six-foot-two teen-ager, Paul David, 18, with real athletic and leadership ability, down to my three-foot-six youngest, Daniel Herbert, 5, there are shared interests, shared conversations, shared learning between us. The same is true with my only girl, Donna Jean, 16, as with James Philip, 14, and Stephen Ernest, 11.

Betty Jane and I are thankful that each of the children has personally accepted Jesus Christ as his Savior except Danny, who is just five. I expect and believe that they will live for Him; but frankly, I have no idea what He has planned for each of them in the way of a vocation. I would not be too shocked if they chose some line of work other than radio. But, of course, it would please me if they decided their place was in missionary radio. I will have to admit that I am human like everybody else! I suppose one of my ideas in having them in Europe for that year was to give them the opportunity of seeing what it was like. But we would feel good seeing the children take up almost any kind of task where their lives can glorify the Lord. I strongly believe that evangelism is a total job to be worked at full-time by the entire body of believers no matter what work a person does. One of the reasons we in the church are doing so poorly in the world is that we have isolated the ministry to a few so-called Christian workers.

Broadcasting out of Tangier continued through December 31, 1959, although we maintained a skeleton staff at Monte Carlo almost from the day the contract was signed the previous September. The new Trans World Radio master plan envisioned eight target areas for our radio programs: 1) Spain and Portugal; 2) British Isles; 3) Scandinavia; 4) Soviet Union; 5) Communist satellite countries; 6) Central Europe; 7) Southern Europe; 8) Middle East and North Africa.

It was our intention to construct a first class system so the radio broadcasts out of Monte Carlo could be beamed deliberately into these target countries. We had a strategic location high on the bluffs of the Southern Alps, overlooking the Mediterranean. From there, the more directionally we would focus our beams, the more effectively we could penetrate each of these language areas.

Our antenna system in Tangier had been a very simple one and we could not direct our programs as efficiently as we would have liked. Now in Monte Carlo we were more than quadrupling our transmitting power, and building elaborate, high-gain curtain antennas with great steel framed towers up to 175 feet high. Each of the Monte Carlo antennas would be composed of four towers, with the "curtain," or network of wires, suspended between two pairs of towers. A reflector made of wire acted like a mirror, causing the majority of power to go in one direction, preventing it from leaking out the back. Our antennas were being arranged in a circular fashion for the simple reason that our target areas lay out from the station in a somewhat circular pattern.

During construction of the antennas the struggles which the workers encountered occasionally assumed the proportions of severe testing. We had realized long before construction had started that a work for God as far-reaching as this one would not escape the notice of Satan. Everything had to be transported in sections up to the top of Mt. Agel. The twenty-one towers to be constructed weighed over ninety tons of metal; and on completion they covered a good share of the suitable available area adjacent to the transmitter building. One day as the men brought up section after section in the wind and snow, one of them actually left his flesh sticking to the cold metal. During the winter, even on the sunny Riviera, it gets bitterly cold in the mountains. Another time one of the trucks went off the road, wrecking it and injuring the driver.

Our completed system gave us one curtain antenna into the Middle East; one into the British Isles; one into Scandinavia; one into Russia; one reversible antenna which reached Spain on one side, and Eastern European countries on the other. These were all equipped with reflectors to add power in the desired direction. In addition, we installed several stack dipole antennas, which with reflectors and directors gave us a good gain into closer countries. One of these was directed into Italy, one into Germany, and one into France.

As we actually began transmitting we ran into other problems. Due north was our most difficult transmitting direction because we had to clear the top of the mountain. Since this made the angle of shooting the beam wrong, the best signal into Scandinavia required construction of an antenna on the other side of the mountain, about a third of a mile away, completely by itself. In many of these installations, it was a matter of trial and error until we found the best combination that would produce an excellent signal into a designated area.

From the beginning we recognized that our programming job would be an intricate one. For even though we had raised our power from 22.5 kilowatts in Tangier to 100 kilowatts in Monte Carlo, we began here with only one transmitter. This meant at first that approximately 500 programs a month which had been sent out over three transmitters in Tangier would somehow have to be rearranged now so they could be transmitted on one. This required the elimination of certain programs so that we could concentrate on broadcasting the most effective ones. However, later a second 100,000 watt transmitter was added.

It was October 16, 1960, when we actually went on the air. We could hardly believe that it was only thirteen months since we signed the agreement with Monte Carlo! Burt Reed and Bill Mial took the tape to the studio that first broadcast night.

Burt says of that first night, "I'll never forget that experience as long as I live. We were there with some of the officials from Monte Carlo, and we just stood around and bawled like babies." It was nine months since the last broadcast from Tangier. Everyone had been working themselves to death—and here it was finally happening! The rest of the Trans World Radio folk were out at Bill's home where we assembled after the broadcasts for a time of thanksgiving and praise.

Missionary Dan Harvey at the radio control panel

Results began to show up almost immediately. During the first year 18,000 letters poured into the station to encourage our hearts; 800 requests came for spiritual help. The results seemed to be in proportion to how much the people in a country had given and worked to make the Gospel broadcast possible in their language. The Trans World Radio policy had been set years before.

Often people ask us, "Do you have people in Monte Carlo to speak all twenty-four languages?" No, this has never been our policy. This would mean that a very limited staff, perhaps one individual, would be doing all the programs for his language group. We want to be able to present a variety of names and voices and program formats to any given country, and the best way to do this is to set up production right there in that country when possible. In this way their local indigenous staff can be responsible for

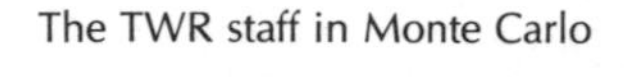
The TWR staff in Monte Carlo

procuring different speakers and musicians, leading evangelicals from all over their area, known and respected by the local listening audience.

For example, O. Hallesby, the Norwegian whose outstanding devotional books on the Christian life are translated into many languages, was a regular speaker over TWR in Monte Carlo. A highly honored and gifted man, Dr. Hallesby taught at the Free University in Norway until his death. He could never have left his position at the University to come to Monte Carlo. But it was quite feasible for the Norwegian engineer to go into the study of this outstanding Christian once a week and record his messages for later airing from Monte Carlo. This was supplemented by the recordings of local church and Bible School choirs. This kind of arrangement gives us both quality and influence which we could never get by trying to do all the production ourselves in one location. By presenting speakers with a clear Gospel message, men who are well-known and loved, we have automatically set the stage for a larger, more receptive audience. And over the years the local support grew steadily until in 1965 half of our support was being met regularly by Europeans.

CHAPTER XIII
GERMANY LEADS THE WAY

Germany, having undertaken tremendous financial backing for its own broadcasts, began to feel a concern for people of other countries. The German Christians were soon supporting missionary broadcasts into Spain, the Middle East, and the Iron Curtain satellites.

Hermann Schulte, who had gotten under the burden of radio evangelism at the very beginning, was proving to be a constant driver. A capable businessman, he not only ran his own business but also operated a Christian bookstore and printing establishment. This gave him an entrée to becoming the first — now largest—producer of Gospel recordings in German. He was so caught up in this whole new chain of events that he almost let his business go in order to make these new ways of sharing his faith in Christ succeed. A very gifted, deeply spiritual man, and member of the Plymouth Brethren group, he is also a testimony in his own home. There he eagerly leads his family in the reading of God's word and praying, not only before each meal, but often afterwards as well.

Giving a substantial part of his time without any remuneration at all, Schulte had organized the German branch of TWR in

Wetzlar, Germany. By telling the broadcast story to individual Christian laymen, to churches, to anyone who would listen, he had gradually enlisted the interest, the prayer, the gifts, and the service of an ever-increasing group of German Christians.

One of the young German men who helped Mr. Schulte was Helmut Gaertner, who for several years headed the office force in Wetzlar. A member of our Tangier staff, Helmut had learned Spanish fluently and was interested in working in the Spanish department. However, when Mr. Schulte started the German branch he asked if we would consider sending Helmut Gaertner to assist him there.

It is difficult to verbalize the sequence of events that led Helmut back to his homeland, for it involved guidance through apparent tragedy that we can never fully grasp with our finite reasoning powers. Helmut had a lovely young wife who suddenly died when her first child was born. We felt this to be total tragedy for him, and we shared with him in the loss. She was a wonderfully dedicated girl, and none of us could reason out her being taken so quickly from us.

At the time of her death in Tangier, it seemed desirable to send Helmut back to Germany for at least a couple of months. He was never one to shirk his duty—he was not only willing to stay on at "The Voice of Tangier," but he expressed his desire to remain on the job. Still we felt it would be good for him to return to his homeland to be with his parents for awhile—to have a clear space in time to adjust to his great loss. It was during this recovery period in Germany that Hermann Schulte asked us if he could use Helmut.

And suddenly Helmut Gaertner, as Schulte's right-hand man, became the real key to the entire German development. Later, God gave him a lovely girl to be his second wife and his loyal assistant in the German work. The Spanish department continued to develop marvelously in Tangier under the leadership of Spaniards Miguel and Maria Valbuena.

Helmut Gaertner had a vital share in making TWR known and heard throughout the land of his birth. His successor, Wilfried Mann, the business manager, is responsible for handling $40,000 a month (as of 1967) that comes in from listeners who are constrained to share in the financial backing of broadcasting God's Word to their own people. A hard worker himself, he leads a strong staff of forty-four full-time workers.

Nowhere have I seen more how God prepares His chosen men for the ministry of TWR than in the life of the program director of our German branch. At the end of World War II, a young man named Horst Marquardt, who was living in the Eastern Zone of Germany, became a zealous student of the Marxist ideology. He joined the Communist party and eventually was appointed to the staff of the East Berlin Radio Station in charge of Communist youth programs and propaganda. Seeing a great contrast between Communist ideology and actual practice, Marquardt became disillusioned and began to read the New Testament. Through the study of the Word he came to a saving knowledge of Christ. Shortly afterwards he made his way to West Berlin. Later he was ordained in an evangelical Methodist Church and became a pastor in Berlin. Still later he went to Vienna, Austria, as a missionary.

During my father's visit in Vienna in 1957 he met Marquardt, who became greatly interested in our broadcast ministry. In 1960 he joined Evangeliums Rundfunk, our German branch, where his outstanding gifts are greatly used and blessed of God.

Gifted members of the production department produce a variety of programs in the Wetzlar branch—evangelistic messages, sermons, dramatic Christian productions, stories, youth and children's programs, question and answer series—all to help create and keep a great body of listeners among the German people, both East and West. Starting by underwriting the cost of airing three programs, the group in Wetzlar has gone on to raise support for fifteen missionary broadcasts a month. Most of these are beamed into countries behind the Iron Curtain, in different languages.

Mr. Schulte reports, "It is from the Eastern Zone of Germany that we receive the most encouragement for our German ministry. People there express immense gratitude through each broadcast message and tell of many changed lives. One time we wanted to determine how effective our noon broadcast really was, and whether we should continue it. In just two weeks more than 2,000 letters and cards arrived, saying, 'Please don't stop the broadcasts—go on with them. We need them.' "

Leaders who started ERF (Evangeliums-Rundfunk) and shared responsibility in the early years. Left to right: Hermann Schulte, Horst Marquardt, and Wilfred Mann

CHAPTER XIV
SPEAKING OF SPAIN

Even after the broadcast facilities were moved to Monte Carlo, Tangier continued to be used as a major production studio. The entire Spanish department remained in North Africa, only sixteen miles — two hours by boat — from the mainland. The lovely property, which belonged to us, housed good recording equipment. It seemed logical that the setup should stay right where it was. The Spanish programs are produced there on tape and airmailed over to Monte Carlo.

Studio facilities in several different countries allow our local radio staffs to keep in close touch with the needs and desires of the people to whom they broadcast. We firmly believe it is absolutely imperative to meet people personally in their own homes in order to relate our programming to genuine heartfelt needs of the listeners.

It has been thrilling to watch God work through the Spanish department—our second largest among the twenty-four language groups. Spain presents one of the greatest opportunities for Gospel broadcasting, since many believers who have little opportunity for Christian fellowship depend almost entirely on their radios for encouragement and spiritual nourishment.

Under the capable direction of Miguel and Maria Valbuena, the Spanish work at the Tangier studio continues to flourish. Miguel and Maria, both well-taught in the Scriptures, are personable individuals, with a lively capacity for good humor and compassion.

Maria, assigned to the Spanish Children's Division, does an admirable job of planning and executing her programs. Known to many thousands of fans as *Tita Maria* (Aunt Maria), she does a dramatic production which attracts adults as well as children to the radio. In fact, even though adults may not wish to admit it, her programs are rated the most popular on the air! These and the other Spanish programs are heard now both from Monte Carlo, during siesta time in the afternoon, and from Bonaire, during the late evening hours.

Miguel is not only an extremely capable Bible teacher, but he

Dr. Freed in an early visit to Spain

also has written several books in Spanish for use in personal Bible study.

Believing thoroughly in the value of person-to-person contact, he has developed a marvelous system of follow-up for listeners who write in to the station. A giant map in his office is studded with colored pins to indicate the location of listeners in over 4,000 villages and towns on the Spanish mainland. Miguel and the staff are also pleased with the interest expressed by many thousands of believers and seekers who have written in to enroll in the Spanish Bible Correspondence Course. This part of the follow-up program supplies national Christians with an instrument for sharing their faith—members often gather neighbors and friends about them in their homes to study the lessons right along with them.

The Valbuenas frequently return from Tangier to Spain in order

Spanish Department Director Miguel Valbuena and his wife Maria looking at a map of Spain

to visit with groups of believers meeting to study and pray—some of whom have found Christ as their Savior through the broadcasts—or with individuals who have special needs. Also, a number of local evangelical pastors stand by to help the Trans World Radio staff with follow-up contacts among interested people in their communities.

Juan Federico, a member of the Spanish staff, travels continuously through Spain on his motorcycle, visiting with people, leading them to Christ, worshiping and praying with them, listening to their joys and their heartaches, and all the time keeping in touch with the pressing human and spiritual needs he finds which can be dealt with through radio programs.

Several factors are kept uppermost in all of our planning and evaluating, no matter which language group we may be considering. Are we really in touch with the people who are sitting in front of their radio sets listening? Do our messages produced in the quiet isolation of our studios really deal with the stress of living in the lonely but busy world of everyday? Are we offering practical help for daily decisions, encouragement for the humdrum attention to duty required of any individual? Are we scheduling the broadcasts at a time when people can listen to them? Are we coming through at the best listening time for those who depend on our fellowship? Are there definite results? We trust the answers are "yes."

To the glory of God we can say that since the beginning of the Spanish broadcasts, more than 50,000 pieces of mail have come in from listeners in Spain. In addition, letters of appreciation continue to arrive from people in twenty-three other countries where Spanish is the official language.

CHAPTER XV FRENCH INTEREST FLARES

The beginning of the French department goes back to Father's residence in Beatenberg, Switzerland, during the period after Mother's death. He had not returned to the work in Tangier after those crisis days, since we had an able young man in charge there. Instead, after a year with my sister and her family in New Jersey, he decided to settle in Beatenberg, where he was always welcomed as a conference speaker, and could also work out of our office there. This arrangement gave him usefulness on his own without giving him the feeling that he was a burden to any of our missionary families.

In March 1960 my father remarried. While living for a period of time at the headquarters of the North Africa Mission in Tangier he met Norah Chambers, a missionary nurse who at the time was engaged as hospital evangelist to the Moorish women patients. She has become a wonderful helpmate to my father and a dedicated worker with our radio staff.

While they were living in Beatenberg, two brothers, graduates of the Beatenberg Bible Institute, came back to the school to attend a conference. They were both evangelists in that little piece of country that has been tossed back and forth from France to

Germany to France—Alsace-Lorraine—but whose people remain basically more German than French. The Buhrer boys had held tent campaigns and made personal visits throughout Alsace-Lorraine, becoming very much at home with the people, who speak a dialect similar to Swiss-German.

The Buhrers came back to Beatenberg as often as possible because of a generous arrangement for graduates of the Bible Institute. With no strings attached, any alumnus may come to the conference center and stay as long as he wants, without its costing him one penny. During one such visit their interest in radio was aroused.

"This would be a wonderful opportunity for France," they said to Father. "There's such a dearth of evangelism there."

Father told them, "We have the facilities, and we would be delighted. I believe we could get a good signal into France with the proper antenna. But somebody has to pay for the program. We don't have unlimited funds to add and add. The money has to be provided."

Robert Buhrer asked, "Would you let me take the responsibility and see what I can do?"

An entire year passed before we heard anything from him beyond that first flare of interest. Back in Beatenberg, he told us that he had enlisted the interest of some French business people in Strasbourg. Again, it was the story of a work that revolved around one man—Buhrer caught the vision of what could be done among the French people. We had talked with many others who were interested, marvelous people thoughout France who cared about reaching other people with God's message. But none of them really got hold of the burden of this particular medium until God touched Robert Buhrer.

At first he appeared a most unlikely person, with only a limited knowledge of French. But he was God's choice. When God's hand fell upon him he became absolutely committed, and through his endless toil the whole French division has become a reality. "Not

Mrs. Norah Freed, who is responsible for the broadcast "Woman to Woman"

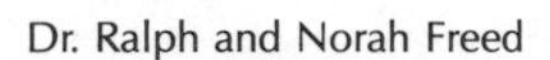

Dr. Ralph and Norah Freed

by might, nor by power, but my spirit, saith the Lord of hosts" (Zech. 4:6). When He calls a man, and that man says yes, there is no limit to what can be accomplished through the power of His Holy Spirit.

Again it was a miracle of God that brought us this man who could do so much. Normally we would think of setting up committees and sub-committees. We would have divided France into more or less equal sectors, with a man in charge of each part. But God's way was to choose one man.

Less than one percent of the French population could be considered even remotely evangelical. With so few actively engaged in the work of the Lord, the burden had always lain heavily on each of them. The same leaders had to serve on most of the boards and committees. "We just do not have the energies and the strength to do all that needs to be done," one explained. "But we are willing to do what we can."

The size of the evangelical community also meant limited financial resources for a program as heavy as the radio broadcasts. But one man—so timid, with no drive apparent—got up and said, "I believe God wants us to do this."

"That's wonderful," retorted the others, "but where are we going to get the funds to go ahead?"

"I don't know. But I do know we have a great God, and I believe He would have us move ahead."

Buhrer gave up his own evangelistic campaigns in order to devote full time to the radio work. In Strasbourg he began contacting people. And once Robert Buhrer began to excite others, the word began to spread like wild fire.

A factory made a certain kind of pressed wood; and Buhrer had the idea that if Christians would collect wood shavings, they could sell them to the factory, and apply the money to the radio expense.

Buhrer went to a doctor and asked, "Is God really blessing you and helping you in your medical practice? If He would give you one

Robert Buhrer, first leader of the French department of TWR

more patient, could you give the income from that new patient to Trans World Radio?"

Another doctor began to mark every fifth patient who came through his door as "the Lord's patient." Whatever that one paid him he gave to the broadcast.

A cabinetmaker made a special cabinet every month, sold it and gave the money for the broadcasts.

To a farmer Buhrer said, "You wouldn't mind giving one of these pigs to the Lord, would you?" When the farmer agreed, he raised that one special pig, and when he sold it, the proceeds went to the TWR French language broadcasts.

Or perhaps he would say, "If the Lord blesses you with larger litters of pigs, would you be willing to give the extra piglets to Him?" When the farmer said, "I'll be glad to," he set aside the income from the sale of the extra hogs for the radio fund.

One gas station attendant gave all the profits from one day's sales each month.

Other people collected cardboard and sold it for money to send to the broadcasts.

Buhrer went from village to village, from city to city, spreading interest and enthusiasm. There was no limit to what God could do with his eagerness.

People who did not have much money brought unpredictable gifts, refuting the saying that "nobody really cares about France." When the Lord leads a heart there is no such thing as a barren country. Pockets loosened up all over the provinces. One elderly person touched by the radio messages wrote, "I want to give a little gift." It was a small sack of coins, 150 twenty-dollar gold pieces—$3,000!

By doing all these unusual things themselves, the French people are able to enjoy daily broadcasts produced and sponsored entirely by their own countrymen. Four or five men in Strasbourg have formed the nucleus. One man in particular gave his big garage for studio space, and the men got together and constructed the facilities, now probably worth between ten and fifteen thousand dollars.

The total cost of putting on programs in French is backed up by individual Frenchmen who not only want to hear the Word of God themselves, but want others to hear it too. An outstanding young French assistant now takes a portable professional tape recorder all over France, recording messages by evangelical speakers for use on the broadcasts. At the studio in Strasbourg the programs are edited by a full-time radio technician, then the tapes are sent to Monte Carlo to be broadcast back into France.

Mr. Buhrer does not speak French too fluently, so he does not speak on the broadcasts. He brings in other men for the messages as he continues to push behind the scenes. Millions of leaflets to make the Gospel programs known have been printed and distributed. Money to bring special speakers to the studio is often raised. More and more programs are being planned and produced. He is a man with a real burden for the French people. The response is constant. Among many others a lady, after hearing the broadcast, accepted Christ as her Savior. She then went out to tell her neighbors about Him. This resulted in their forming daily prayer groups. Now in her area a number of different groups meet each day of the week to pray for the French broadcasts. And so the effect of the work multiplies.

CHAPTER XVI MONITORS FOR EUROPE

After things were rolling at the new station we saw the need of consolidating the European work in one place. We dissolved the Swiss office and moved the headquarters (office) to Monte Carlo. After several branch offices were set up, the objectives of the central headquarters took on a whole new aspect. Among other important functions it became the focal point of all our signal testing.

To determine how well we were getting through to the target areas, we would send out a regular broadcast signal—music with a recurring spot announcement: "This is a test broadcast coming to you from Trans World Radio." Then we would spot test listeners in the various countries, or we would make monitoring trips into the different locations. We needed to know not only where the signal was best picked up, but also when it was satisfactory. We were interested in finding out how strong it was, what type of interference we encountered, or if there were any interferences on a given frequency. If so, we needed to find another frequency that would provide a clear channel.

No place is completely devoid of interference. It is a case of getting on a frequency which can reach into the target area with a consistently good signal. But it is a problem that is never solved all at once and forever—we have to keep checking to see that we are being heard clearly. A sudden change can be brought on by another station unexpectedly appearing right on our frequency. Sometimes the new station is not as strong as we are, so *it* will have to look for another spot on the dial.

As a result of this problem we have developed a network of monitors all over Europe, evaluating the signal, giving daily reports to us so we can know immediately when any frequency or other problem develops. We may find it necessary to act rapidly so that the very next night we reappear on a different frequency. We do try to inform our listening audience of such a change before we put it into effect, although this is not always practical.

Here actually is the most acute problem we have to face—simply finding a place on the correct meter band with a minimum of interference. Our whole project rests on the success we have in getting through clearly to our listeners. We can program magnificently and constantly, but we go no farther than the studio ceiling if the listening conditions are not right. Frequency and propagation create the field of our biggest battle. In Monte Carlo we struggled constantly for two years before we achieved any degree of finesse at all. It was a fantastic ordeal—reaching consistently with a good signal into our many target areas in Europe, North Africa, the Middle East, and behind the "Iron Curtain." Most of us bore the scars of those hard-driving days for a long time.

As Trans World Radio became widely known, young people in all parts of the States and Canada began to apply to us for missionary service. From the very beginning we realized that in such work as ours we needed highly trained specialized workers. Yet we have scrupulously followed the principle that each candidate must show the highest spiritual standards and a genuine call of God for a lifetime service on the mission field.

Here again I can testify to the faithfulness of our God. At the time of the closing of the Tangier station we had twenty-six full-time workers on the field. Most were transferred to Monte Carlo. Today there are thirty-five missionary workers serving the Monte Carlo station, recording studios, and offices under the leadership of my father. Eugene Priddy is field secretary in charge of administration and Norman Olsen, station manager, is responsible for the technical operations. They are assisted by Roy Hertzog, chief engineer, Dave Carlson, director of publicity and public relations, and Lee Vandervort, field treasurer. They all testify to the Lord's wonderful leading, to His full provision, and to the joy of serving Him in the close team-work which the ministry of missionary radio requires. At the beginning of 1967 the total Trans World Radio family of United States and Canadian missionaries and the many national workers in our various European and Middle East branches for whose support we are directly or indirectly responsible—consisted of over 200 adults and nearly 150 children. We have a great God!

The work was expanding in several directions. Some of the outstanding businessmen in Norway, who had been responsible for that first payment to Monte Carlo, were still moving ahead. They had established a good recording studio in Oslo, with a wonderful variety in the programs they produced. One man now spends his full time traveling throughout the country recording messages and music by talented people of God. Others work long hours every day putting them together in their studio. These are sent to Monte Carlo where they go on the air, and are beamed back to Norway.

Letters give evidence that the programs are picked up by Danes and Finns as well, and a Swedish language program also brings results. In Scandinavia many letters come from "people of the sea" who have been encouraged and blessed as they pick up the broadcasts on board ship.

In Great Britain attention to the broadcasts is steadily expanding. Radio expense looks very high there, but we are beaming a number of American-produced programs to the British and their interest is assuring. Beginning to catch a vision, they are now producing some effective programs of their own. Northern Ireland has had a happy development. A couple of businessmen who have been listening to Trans World Radio for several years are now producing the Irish Gospel Hour and are financially underwriting it through a circle of interested Irish Christians. The potential in Britain is some fifty-five million people.

On the verge of suicide, a young Englishman—overwhelmed by his problems—hesitated long enough to turn on his favorite radio program. Just a hair's breadth from that station, the sound of singing pushed its way through the crowded band. Trans World's 100,000 watts of power bestowed a different kind of music on him—songs his mother had sung to him years before. He tuned them in clearly, and the message of the Gospel began to touch the heavy ache in his heart. Instead of taking his life, he gave it to the

Equipment arriving at Monte Carlo transmission site, Mount Agel

Lord Jesus Christ. Enough power to thrust the words of life through the babble of a dozen stations made all the difference in the world.

In the privacy of their own homes people listen to missionary radio—people around the world who would have no other way of being brought into God's fellowship to learn of love and forgiveness. More people than we will ever know listen and respond to the voice of God as they sit—unpressured, unseen before their radios.

Over in Portugal a lady wrote, "Your radio programs have completely changed my life." She explained that she was brought up to believe that she had to work her way to heaven, and that she had been diligently doing just that. Desperately through her attempts to be good she kept trying to find some assurance of her salvation. Then one day, turning the dial of her radio, she heard a Gospel program in Portuguese from Monte Carlo. The fear and desperation in her heart were replaced by thankfulness to the Savior, as she discovered that He had already paid the price of her salvation. She told in her letter to us how she had put her trust in Jesus Christ. Then through the follow-up program of Trans World Radio we put her in touch with an evangelical church, and she was baptized one month later.

"Now I have assurance that my sins are gone," she wrote again, "and I have peace with God. I tell everybody about Christ. I'm so grateful for your Gospel programs from Monte Carlo."

A shepherd boy, tending his sheep all alone on a hillside in Corsica, listened to Trans World Radio on his little transistor radio. He gave his heart to Christ and later moved on to the nearby island of Sardinia as a "foreign" missionary—telling others of the Shepherd who loves and saves beyond all human hopes. Jesus said, "Go ye into all the world and preach the Gospel to every creature." That we might "go" and "preach" is the hard-core purpose of every program beamed from Trans World Radio "into all the world."

CHAPTER XVII
BLANKETING THE MIDDLE EAST

The Middle East, of course, is of great personal concern and interest to us, since our family lived there for so many years. We were particularly eager to get started on Arabic language broadcasts because we could so easily visualize the people who would hear. These were the people both Father and I knew from long, first-hand experience. During the many years of our missionary assignment in Palestine and Syria, we had chafed under the desire to reach more of the Arabs for Christ than we possibly could in person. Father's ministry to the people in scores of villages had been a fruitful one. However, neither of us ever got away from the underlying fact that the number of untouched people would always far exceed those we were reaching. You can imagine how thrilled we were with the prospect of radio penetrating into places where we never had time or opportunity to go ourselves. Our vision for the Arabic people was vivid, for they were in a special way our own, and it gave us such a burden as we attempted to raise support for the airing and production of these particular broadcasts. When a person has this sort of personal concern for others he always wants to do far more than he is able to do. This was the case in the familiar and beloved Middle East as we started to plan.

Although Father's principal work was with the Arabs, Hebrew programs were also very vital. When Israel became a nation, this brought about a total separation between the Hebrew and Arabic departments. The Hebrew story precedes that of the Arabic broadcast.

During the centuries of dispersion, the Jewish people have often spoken Yiddish, a German dialect in Hebrew characters. One of their strong desires as the Jews returned to Israel as a nation was to restore the Old Testament Hebrew language to daily use. This determination, which began around 1920, culminated in 1948 when Hebrew was designated the official language of communication and education.

The Jewish people have a special respect for those Jews whose roots go down into Palestine several generations. Such was the

Dr. Jacob Blum, first Hebrew broadcaster of the Hebrew department of TWR

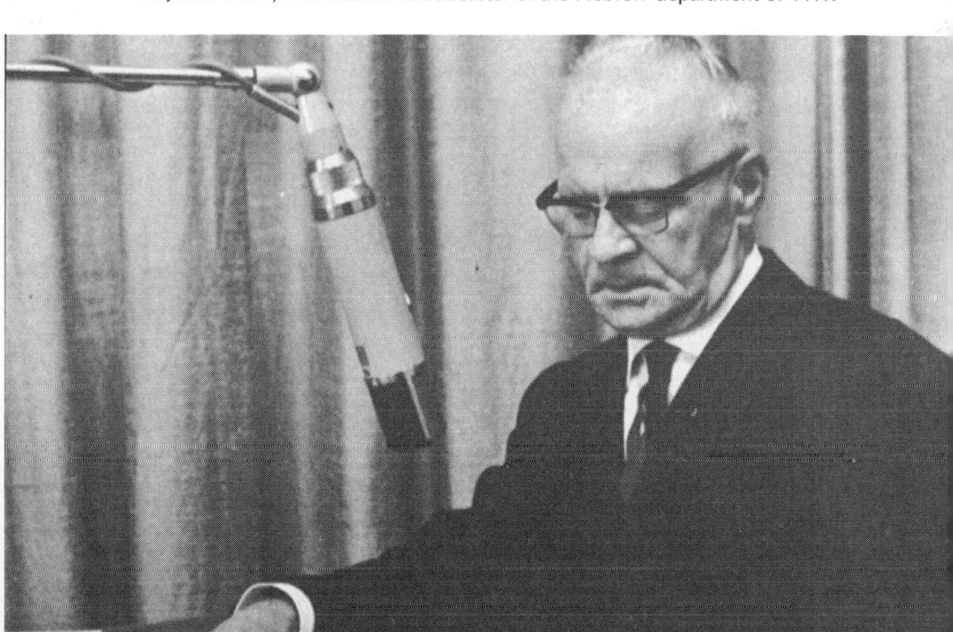

kind of man whom God chose for us in the Middle East. He was a Hebrew, born near Tiberias, who spoke Hebrew proficiently from childhood on. This man, Jacob Blum, thirsty for education, went to Holland in the early '30's to study. During this period he was converted, one of the few Jews won to Christ before the British mandate. He earned two doctoral degrees, one in chemistry and one in the field of theology. His great desire to return with the Gospel to his own people in Palestine eventually came about under the auspices of some Holland Christians who sent him back to his homeland as a missionary.

Some time later when the American Messianic Fellowship in the United States became interested in broadcasts for Israel, they began sponsoring Dr. Blum in a daily Hebrew program and faithfully continued until his death in September 1966. Dr. Blum

Dick Olson in TWR's Beirut studio

came to Monte Carlo once a year to record his messages. Then the staff edited, added the music, and finalized the programs for broadcast into the Middle East.

One of the listeners from Israel tells how much he hated Dr. Blum at first because "you were an apostate from our religion and nation and went over to the camp of our enemies who wanted to destroy us . . . I was the most furious opponent and the fiercest fighter against Christian missions . . . until the time I heard your radio program. Please tell me when we can meet and where . . . one of the coffee houses will be fine."

One man to whom Dr. Blum had spoken many times suddenly became ill. When Dr. Blum arrived at the hospital the man was already in a coma. He prayed that the Lord would allow him to speak to this man once more before he entered eternity. Shortly afterwards the man opened his eyes and said, "Is that you, Dr. Blum? I believed you would be here—that you wouldn't let me die alone. Your witness to me has not been in vain. I am ready to die because I now know I am going to my Messiah, my Redeemer."

Our keen interest in the Arab-speaking world was implemented as we prayed earnestly for the right man and the right opening. The contact that came to light for Arabic broadcasts is another example of God's marvelous designs. Father had been impressed during the '20s with a zealous young man from Australia who was sitting under him for his Arabic language examination. Years later, when this same Keith Stevenson heard about Trans World Radio, he got in touch with us. At the time he had established a literature mission in Beirut, Lebanon, under the auspices of Christians in Australia. As a subsidiary undertaking, he had begun making recordings to take around to shut-ins. His real gift for planning programs and his high standards of production led us to negotiate with him, first when he came to Switzerland, and later when I went out to Beirut to visit him. The outcome of our discussions was the incorporating of his Gospel Recording Society as our Trans World Radio branch for the Middle East. Rallying round him several gifted Christian Arabic speakers, Mr. Stevenson produced programs with a superb quality and positive message. He furthermore volunteered to establish the complete studio facility in Beirut for the production of programs in Arabic, Armenian, and Turkish.

From one listener in the United Arab Republic—among the most challenging of Trans World Radio's targets—comes this encouraging letter:

"I rejoice to tune daily to your broadcast and feel secure when I am near the radio listening to your messages which direct me in the right path. I ask you to point me to the way which leads to the great end by giving me information about the Lord Jesus. Also, please give me questions to encourage me to read the Bible and some of the hymns which are sung on your program."

The whole activity among the Arabs continues to enlarge. Dick and Jeanne Olson, one of our finest couples, have gone to Beirut with their children to head up the work there. Dick spent several years under my father in Monte Carlo. He also was a very effective worker in Bonaire. Under God the work continues to grow. Dick is assisted by Jad Dally, a devoted and capable national of Jordan.

The story of Jacob Jambazian, who manages the Armenian department in Beirut, also goes back to the early days we spent in Jerusalem. Many years ago when Armenian refugees came from Turkey, a Christian family opened an orphanage in Jerusalem. As a young boy in that orphanage, Jacob Jambazian listened to my father speak to the children. Years later, following his graduation from Bible School in Beatenberg, he and father met again.

The history of the Armenians is a strange one. They have been a nation for 2725 years, but have lived as minority groups in many lands not their own. Hundreds of thousands of them are clannishly clustered in Arab countries—maintaining their own schools in their own proud language. The ministry of God's Word in their language is very effective among them; they thrill to hearing the Gospel in their mother tongue.

The southeastern tip of Communist Russia is full of Armenians.

Armenian broadcaster Jacob Jambazian and his wife Knar

Russia appeals to their nationality, claiming to organize a nation for them. More than half a million Armenians have been wooed into the independent Armenian Soviet Republic in the Caucasian area. Jambazian is preparing several programs a week, by tape for broadcasting to his people, with encouraging results.

Trans World Radio aims to be a service organization, granting to indigenous peoples a voice to tell of Jesus Christ to their own people. This is how it all began in Iran. In 1962 Dick Corley of International Missions, Inc., sat down to talk with one of our workers at a conference in Chicago. He thought the Persian people would profit from a Gospel program in their language, and he wondered what he could do to get one started. We encouraged him to get a good tape recorder to take back with him so he could prepare a trial program in Persian.

The next thing we knew we received a tape in the mail from Iran, with instructions accompanying it. Corley wanted it to go on the air by eight o'clock in the morning in Iran. This meant we had to talk the crew in Monte Carlo—two time zone hours west—into getting up an hour earlier than usual so they could play the Persian tape at 6:00 A.M. This was in December 1962. Since then the Director of International Missions, Elrey Larow, has counted between 7,000 and 8,000 Persians enrolled in the radio-promoted Bible correspondence course. He credits the radio program with drawing 95 percent of these new Bible students.

The Lord continues to perform new miracles in Monte Carlo. On April 1, 1966, Trans World Radio was granted permission to use Radio Monte Carlo's giant 400,000 watt medium wave (standard broadcast) AM transmitter after 10:00 P.M. This unbelievable breakthrough opens up a vast number of previously unreached homes in the heart of Europe during prime evening hours. The impact and effect of this new outreach literally defies imagination. Only eternity will reveal the countless thousands of additional hearts that will be reached in this way. Truly we have a great God.

CHAPTER XVIII
A NEW ERA FOR TRANS WORLD RADIO

In June 1961 we returned to the States from France. Construction of the large complex of broadcast facilities at Monte Carlo had been very difficult, but I had found the challenge most enjoyable. That is one of my problems—I really *enjoy* hard work. The harder the work, the more push and drive it takes, the more interesting it is to me. We knew the Lord had helped us. It was a tremendous task and a very great strain. We felt we had successfully completed a good thing. Betty Jane and the children and I came back to America by ship to give us a chance to unwind.

A few days in the office in Chatham preceded a visit to Betty Jane's parents and some special meetings in North Carolina. The suitcases were not even unpacked yet when Ben called to suggest a little time for recreation. I jumped at the chance to join Ben and a couple friends for a Saturday round of tennis. I loved the game—had even won some city tennis tournaments in earlier years. The four of us had played off and on for years, and had quite a warm little rivalry going among us. Merle Daugherty, a commercial artist from North Plainfield, was a man about sixty-five years of age. His first thought when Ben called him was that he had a heart problem and perhaps should not play. But when he heard we were shaping up for doubles, he let his eagerness get the better of him since doubles, he assured his wife, would be less strenuous. Harold Mathisen, an investment broker, was a neighbor of ours, as well as a member of Long Hill Chapel, the church we attend.

Harold plays tournament tennis, and Merle is an old war horse on the court. He has two rackets—one he says is crooked and he uses it only when he has "blood in his eye."

Ben and I were standing Harold and Merle and we had played two sets, each of us winning one. The third set was completely different—not the normal easygoing volley we had started out with. The play became extremely competitive—Harold was slamming the ball neatly into the far corner, and Merle had picked up his winning racket. Every stroke was crucial. After twenty-two games the set was still tied. They would win a game, then we would win one. I don't think we ever finished the set. Darkness fell and we had to stop because we couldn't see what we were doing.

I noticed quite a bit of fatigue while we were playing but I attributed it to the fact that I had not played for a long time. Basically I was in good health. Just that morning Paul and Jim had said, "Daddy, you sure look strong!"

I was. I flexed my muscles for them and they grinned. I felt great.

But when we stopped playing I realized I was very tired. I felt dizzy and strange. I opened the door and sat down in Harold's car as we wound up the conversation under the streetlight. I didn't say much. Even after Harold and I drove away from the courts and past the hospital I let him talk, but I could hardly answer—or even think of anything but my own misery. The thought crossed my mind that maybe I ought to have him stop at the hospital and drop me off. Maybe I needed a good checkup.

When we arrived home, I ran to the house. "I feel miserable!" I told my wife. I figured it was indigestion; I had had it several times on ship board, and many times before that when I was going at a hard pace.

Betty Jane put her arm around me and helped me up the stairs and onto the bed. I did not want to frighten her unduly, but suddenly a terrible pain hit me. I felt fantastic pressure as though a steel band were being tightened around my chest.

Between groans and sharp explosions of pain I was able to tell her, "This isn't anything ordinary, honey. You've got to call Bob right away!" My wife couldn't believe I really needed a doctor, and I could hardly bear the pain of telling her. Dr. Robert Francis, a close personal friend and a wonderful Christian, had returned home from his day off only five minutes before Betty Jane phoned.

The few minutes before anything happened seemed like an eternity. I was sure I was dying. I told my wife that I loved her, and I wanted to see the children. They had been sleeping but had wakened because of all the excitement. She gathered the four of them—Paul, Donna, Jim, and Stevie—in the bedroom, and I told them I loved them and that more than anything else I wanted them to live for the Lord. I told them all goodby. I was sure this was it.

The rescue squad and ambulance arrived at the house just ahead of the doctor. I could hardly breathe. I was perspiring terribly. I had pains all down my arms. They immediately clapped the oxygen mask over my face, and then I was aware that Dr. Bob Francis was also bending over me with a hypodermic needle. He was quite sure it was a heart attack. As they carried me down the stairs and lifted the stretcher into the ambulance, I could see the children standing alone and scared in the doorway. I was sure I would never see them again. Sometime afterwards I learned that one of the policemen from the rescue squad had come back to the house to stay with the children. Later a neighbor lady came in and took them home with her. Betty Jane followed me to the hospital, but I was not able to talk with her.

For three days I was in an oxygen tent. The big strong daddy so proud of his muscles in the morning, the hard-driving radio builder used to working fifteen hours a day seven days a week, had been knocked down. All of a sudden I could not even feed myself, not even lift an arm. I was flat on my back, and for one long month I was not to move from that hospital bed.

After a week the test confirmed the fact that I had had a straight heart attack—a coronary thrombosis—but with little permanent damage. Frankly, I found it hard to accept the fact. I did not really believe it could happen to me. I was only forty-two years of age and otherwise very healthy. But I kept telling myself, "Dr. Francis *must* be right. If he is right then I should do what he says."

I followed to the letter every detail of his instructions. He was most patient and understanding. His life and testimony meant much to me during that difficult time. I never consciously deviated one iota from his directions. First, I went down from 209 pounds to 160 pounds. Then on a special diet I went back up to 172—where I should stay. Even now I do not stray from my diet, and I still manage a half hour rest practically every afternoon.

During this time of quiet the Lord searched me through and through. I had never had so much time with Him—to read His Word, to listen to Him, to talk with Him, and to read the writings of those who knew Him well. Before, I had thought I had been running things. I used to imagine that if I was not around to keep my finger on everything in our radio work, on any given day, something awful would happen. Now I had to realize that if anything would happen, I would not even know about it, let alone discuss it and find a solution! Suddenly I realized that nobody—not *anybody*—is indispensable to God's work. And I became aware that God's work would continue without any one of us. The only indispensable thing for a Christian is to be in the center of the will of God for his life.

After leaving the hospital I could hardly stand up. The first week I could go up only one or two steps before I had to sit down to rest. For one whole month I was confined to the house, then for another month I had the privilege of going outside the house. Then the doctor really shook me up when he told me I could not drive an automobile for three months! Well, I could not believe that! But the doctor stared me down saying, "It doesn't make any difference, Paul. That's it!"

"But who's going to drive?" I stammered.

"Your wife will," he matter-of-factly answered.

"But she makes me nervous!" I complained.

Laughing at me he said, "You'll just have to go ahead and get nervous then."

I will never forget the first time my wife and I went out to dinner after the hospital experience. Since then I have come to realize that the place we chose is a very quiet spot as restaurants go. But when I stepped into that place, the normal hubbub sounded like the roar of Niagara Falls beating down on me. I could not stand it, and after ten or fifteen minutes I quit trying and told Betty Jane we would have to go home.

I just thought I would never be able to face people again. I had been so alone for so long. There had been no visitors allowed in the hospital—with two or three exceptions. At home there was only my immediate family. One of the most difficult things I had to face was speaking in public again.

As I gradually got my strength back I accepted a speaking engagement in a little church not far from our home. I was actually scared to death! Normally I had enjoyed talking to a crowd. I had done it countless times in English and through interpreters in many lands. To stand before people and witness for the Lord was something I had always enjoyed. But this time I was afraid I would not make it. I was afraid I would fall over, afraid I would forget what I was saying, afraid that something—I didn't know what—would happen.

The Lord impressed upon me that I must keep my thoughts on Him—not be thinking of myself. When I stood up I was able to bring a short simple message straight from my heart. It gave me unspeakable joy and encouragement to know that I could once again do this. From that first night it was easier to go on until, eventually, it all seemed normal once again.

For all practical purposes I died that day I had the attack, because I was sure I was not going to live. The doctor had convinced me of the seriousness of my condition, and to me it was as though it were the finish of my life. The ensuing days became a time of reevaluation, of seeing things that had not been done that should have been done. I was impressed that I had not put first things first. At the beginning my mind had no release from the continuous thought: I should have done this, I should have worked harder at that, why didn't I get at that other thing? But as I prayed and read God's Word one thought loomed constantly above all others: "Was each day one hundred percent committed to Jesus Christ? Was my life in the center of His will for me?" I used to think, "Maybe I should have built a bigger station. Maybe the staff should have been larger. Perhaps I should have organized the work differently." Out of these first quick thoughts the real issue crystallized—the renewal of my own commitment to the Lord each day.

Later the doctor faced me with the possibility that I might have to change my whole way of life. This made me aware of the fact that maybe I would not be able to do very much—maybe God would even want me in some totally different ministry, and operate the radio work without me. Again I saw that total commitment to Him was essential, and while I was recuperating I gained a new understanding of commitment of my life to Him. This led to a real crisis decision—the realization that everything must be of God, not of ourselves. As a result, I can say that God has done what has been done in this work, and the more we rely on Him, the more He can accomplish.

I think it is a real mistake, however, for one to turn around and say, "Ever since then I have done exactly what I promised the Lord." I know from my own experience that we are human, we are frail. And I would be terribly reluctant to say that I had been totally committed ever since that turning point in the hospital. Nevertheless, each day I am conscious that there is one thing needful for my day: I must give it to Him; I must be centered in His desire for me.

The experience of having to yield control of myself and my work changed my pattern of thinking a great deal. It taught me really to search the Word, not depending on my own physical strength, but on the Word of God for food. I had a new understanding of what it meant to depend, not on myself, but on the Lord. Many of us Christians who are doing interesting jobs that are important to us believe success is just a matter of moving on ahead. By lip service I always had said, "We must trust the Lord for this, and God helps us with that." But I did not really behave as though total dependence on Him is essential.

During this hospital experience I also learned something about my attitude toward others. I used to think it was the thing to work ten, twelve, even fifteen hours a day, seven days a week. The most important concern of my life was to work, keep moving, drive myself to get one job done and to start another. Anyone who worked less than I went down in my book as a slacker. I was unsympathetic, intolerant. Life was not given to us for play, I argued; we need to work. At forty-two years of age, struck down suddenly by a heart attack, I slowly shifted my views. I began to be tolerant of other people's capacities and gifts, other people's decisions.

At the same time I was learning how my attitudes towards others—and towards myself—fell short, I could do little to stop the thought wheels that constantly turned in my mind. Even on the third day after the attack—while I was still under oxygen tent, my mind raced ahead to develop plans for enlarging Trans World Radio through the addition of a strategic station in the Caribbean area. I had been told by that time that I would be flat on my back for at least a month, so I asked Ben and others to be my hands and feet. As a matter of fact, we had heard of a very interesting transmitter for sale in Cincinnati, Ohio. Operated by WLW for the U. S. Government's Office of War Information, it had played a powerful part in the psychological warfare during World War II. This was one of the chief instruments used to beam the American story into enemy territory in an attempt to counteract strong Nazi propaganda. Hitler was so well aware of the importance of this transmitter—and the damage it was doing to his cause—that he dubbed it "The Cincinnati Liar."

We bought it for a fraction of its original value. Before it ever went into use, however, we sold it to clear the way for newer, better equipment. Thus, even though this station was never used, it seems the hand of the Lord worked on our behalf through the acquisition. For it was this move that started the wheels turning for the establishment of a super-power station outside the continent of Europe.

There is no question in our minds—Betty Jane's and mine—that all the circumstances of the heart attack were lined up by God. I cannot express in words how much my wife meant to me during those days. She went through the whole thing with me, encouraged me in every little detail, helped me spiritually at a time when I desperately needed understanding. It is no easy thing for an active man to be taken completely out of the work he had founded and nurtured, to be brought down to absolutely nothing. But that's exactly what happened to me. So often my own inclination had been to run ahead, to drive a thing to its ultimate conclusion so I could have the satisfaction of seeing it happen. But now I was learning exactly the opposite truth from the heart attack, "Be still and know that I am God."

Betty Jane has been one hundred percent with me in sickness and in health. I do not think this work could ever have become a reality, nor could I have gone through the things I have, without her deep Christian devotion as a wife and the faithful mother of our five wonderful children. My wife holds that God lined up all the details of that significant evening so my life could be spared. She is thoroughly convinced, and does not yield an inch to anyone else who might say something to the contrary. She actually believes that tennis match saved my life. The doctor told us that I had been living at a terrible pace. She feels if I had not brought on the attack through the energy output during the tennis match, the condition that already existed in my heart would have gradually become worse, bringing on a massive and perhaps fatal attack later.

Friends and relatives watching on the sidelines have commented to me that while the heart attack did not essentially change the thrust of my ministry, nevertheless it seemed to place the entire work in a new perspective—the perspective of eternity. For the first time the long range aspect of the radio work came into focus. Nothing materially changed from the point of view of the direction—we continued to pursue the same objectives—but there was a new urgency about the task, a new dependency on God. It seemed to thrust us into a new era.

CHAPTER XIX FROM BETTY JANE

Because my wife feels God has taught her important lessons too, through my period of illness, Betty Jane has asked if she could borrow a couple pages here for a special message to wives and sweethearts:

"The Lord had a lesson for me through Paul's heart attack. Back in 1948 I had such a hard time letting Paul go off by himself to Switzerland. We had never been separated, and I did not like the idea at all. It was at that time that I had my first struggle over really giving my husband to God.

"I had done this many times before with other things. It is not so hard to do without this or that, but when you have someone whom you love very much, and you are called on to give up that person—that is the acid test. Letting him go out of your grasp is the most heart-rending experience for a woman. I found that giving my husband to the Lord was the most difficult thing I had ever done—to really take my hands off his life, to be willing to be separated from him, to accept his being away from me. I suppose actually the difficulty arises from the realization that I was not first in his life. Of course, I would have always *said* that I wanted the Lord to be first with him, but *saying* it and *acting* it are oceans apart.

"His trip to Beatenberg shortly after we were married was just a tiny little test in comparison to all that has happened since. But in my young life and in my tender heart it was a terribly big thing at that time for me to give my assent to something that took us away from each other. Through the pain of separation the Lord was teaching me a lesson we all must learn—not to cling too tightly to the dearest things He has given us. Since then my story has been keyed to that one lesson—just letting Paul go. I've learned I cannot outgive God. No matter what we give to Him, He always gives back more—always.

"The night of Paul's heart attack, it was as though I was being called on the carpet by God. Did I really mean what I had said so many years before? After all, God had a right to take him—for I had given Paul back to Him. I was sure that He would not make a mistake with Paul. Reviewing the history of our companionship, I faced losing him. I hardly slept at all the first night my husband was in the hospital. I could not see how God would want to take him home when he was so important to so many of us in the family and the work. But then I also knew that no man is indispensable. My thinking finally focused down to the covenant I had personally made with the Lord earlier—Thy will be done, no matter what the cost.

"Even facing with great certainty the possibility of Paul's being taken from me that night, I felt the quieting hand of the Lord through it all. I knew He surely would work out His will.

"The next couple of weeks put me to another kind of test. Paul had made it through the night, and it appeared God did not intend to take him home at this point. He was lying flat on his back, and the doctor said that he would have to stay there that way at least a month. But no, Paul could not lie there, content to just get well! The third day he began talking about starting another radio station—one in the Caribbean! He was asking others to go around and do the research. But Paul was actually pushing the expansion almost before he was out of sedation!

"Well, this made me—in the flesh—hit the ceiling! I thought, 'My! Haven't we had enough? Lying there on his death bed, he's talking about starting another station. Don't we matter to him? We need him, too.'

"I was violently opposed to Paul's thinking about work—lying there in the hospital, the week after his attack. Flat on his back, he still was busy. He was not supposed to get upset at all. He was supposed to have complete rest. Yet he was starting the wheels turning for 'a station of our own'—that's what he called it. In Monte Carlo we had leased the transmitters and antennas. I could not see why all this had to happen right now. Why not five years from now? I really felt it meant his life.

"It wasn't that I had been against a new station, for I too wanted to see him own his own powerful station in the Caribbean. But I was against the timing. I really looked at the starting of another huge project as the death of Paul. Then I saw it was once again a case of my not having given Paul—and his far-reaching ideas, and his reservoir of drive—completely over to God.

"This was a difficult struggle for me, and for three or four months I did all I could to discourage Paul in his new research. Since I seemed to be making little progress with him, I decided I had better have it out with the Lord. I finally got to the place where I was able to say, 'All right Lord, if this is really what You want, it may mean his death, but this is the way it will have to be.'

"In spite of all the personal loss I anticipated I finally had to face the fact that Paul was first of all God's man, and God was the one who was ordering his steps. At that point I began once again to pull with my husband. From that time on, it became easier for me to trust the Lord for all the progress as we entered the preparation stages for a station in the Caribbean.

"The main push toward the completion of the new station came from Paul's belief that he might not have much time to live. *It put an urgency into his living–everything* had to be done immediately. We talk so often about the Lord's coming back, and how we must work quickly. But it is not so real to us until there is a possibility that life is going to be over any minute. Really none of us can know beyond the next heart beat; essentially, the uncertainty of life is the same for every man. But a heart attack makes this knowledge an actual recognition—that we are just a heart beat from eternity. Paul and I live constantly in the light of another attack. Some nights neither of us sleep because he has pain, and we wonder if this is it. But through it all there is a deep peace that our lives are in the Lord's hands.

"The brush with death also caused many little things that were not essential in our lives to look quite different to me. For instance, now I use my good silver, we enjoy music, we go places and do things together. You might say, now we do things before it's too late, instead of just talking about doing them. For one thing, I do not just keep on doing the dishes when I could be sitting with him listening and talking together!

"Really he seems to do more and go harder than he ever did. But now he goes about it in a better way–*he paces himself so as to cut the strain, and I feel it is my duty to help him with this.* He is not able to care so much any more about racing to be on time for an appointment—the minute he saves might be just the strain that induces another attack. He also takes more time for the children—to help them with their homework, or their baseball and football, to be with them and to do the things that really count with them, things that will make lasting memories for them. Before, he often would say, 'Don't bother Daddy, I'm busy on the phone.' Now he listens to the many little details so important in their lives; he takes time to counsel them. In a sense, in giving him up to God, we have found him.

"It is fantastic the amount of drive Paul has. This sometimes causes burdens, frustration, even heartaches to those who are close to him and want to keep pace with him. I don't know how he keeps going. I fell by the wayside long ago. All I can really do is to keep the home fires burning. He keeps telling me that is the thing he needs—the assurance that I am pulling with him quietly and confidently. That keeps him going, with confidence and peace of heart and mind.

"He tells me often, 'Honey, if there's no strife at home, if you're not upset and irritable and at cross purposes, that's what really helps me.' Is this so big a thing to do for the dearest person in life to me?

"All these new insights give me a new way of looking at life. I seem always to be asking when a choice comes up, 'Will I wish I had done this if there is never a chance to do it again? Or will I be glad I chose not to do it?' When I know the answer, then I go ahead

Dr. Paul Freed's family, Chatham, New Jersey, mid-1960s

and act accordingly. I analyze everything I do to keep from wasting time and energy on something needless. I want to make everything count for the Lord. It is almost as though now I look at life more from the end than from the beginning—sort of in retrospect. It helps me to understand what God would want me to do."

CHAPTER XX
SUPER-POWER IN THE CARIBBEAN

The faster the minutes tick by the more positive I become that God has His own timeclock!

When we lag behind His schedule, or try to shove out ahead of Him, the alarm is sure to go off to warn us. That is what happened that day in August when God stopped me—suddenly! I believe it was God who rang the bell—and for several reasons: among others, to teach me deep truths, and to provide a powerful means of penetrating far corners that had never been reached with His truth.

It was necessary for me to gain thinking and praying time for my own life, as well as for the new radio expansion. So He stopped me.

In the hospital I had no idea how many more days were left in my life. Somehow I felt much was still to be accomplished. I just had not done enough for the Lord.

For a long time we had wanted to find a supplementary spot for broadcasting into Europe, and the experts had told us it should be in the Caribbean area. Now it became urgent that the search get started. This phase of the work did not move fast. It emerged through deep prayer and long hours of struggle, at a time when everything was not only an effort but a risk.

My dear wife loved me so much she did not want me to *think* about anything—especially a staggering new project! But I was quietly conscious within myself that this move would not be a matter of struggle—even if I had the energy to push it through. I knew the new plans would have to be full-term plans—planted and nurtured by God, and born in much prayer and intelligent thought. I prayed, and Betty Jane prayed. And we were not always praying with the same emphasis, for she so wanted to keep me *safe*, and I wanted to give my all.

During this time when I was recuperating, I became aware that I was geared to two kinds of thinking. Some of my best and clearest thinking is done when I am alone. Since my heart attack I have noticed especially that when I am waking up from my afternoon nap my mind is very clear on certain things I need to consider. But on other matters I seem to need to shape the thoughts into words out loud. When this is the case I am grateful for my wife. She has been a wonderful listener—very much interested in helping me formulate my pieces of thought into workable procedures. Through the months of searching and planning for an additional site, it has meant more than I can say to talk to her and have her share many of my burdens and desires and heartfelt needs.

Further reading prepared me. When I saw what God had done with other men who were His disciples, I got a vision of my own life. I saw myself coming up short. I recognized the vastly increasing numbers of people who needed to hear the Gospel. I remembered the technicians who had informed us of the best location. These perceptions mingled in my heart and mind. And it was actually during the three months when I was ordered to do nothing that God's clock indicated it was nearly time to move.

I found myself in a delicate situation. Before God, I felt there was much to be done. Before my family, I felt I needed to use every precaution to follow the doctor's instructions. It took a lot of devotion and consideration on Betty Jane's part, and a lot of patience and prayer on mine to work out the details for each day.

The three month's restrictive period was up shortly after Christmas, 1961. In February 1962 I was on my way to Puerto Rico to look over the possibilities there for a super-power station. Ben Armstrong accompanied me. He and his wife Ruth joined us full-time in 1959. He served faithfully as director of radio, establishing effective cooperative relations between Trans World Radio and many evangelical broadcasters of the United States and Canada. Ben and Ruth also served a year at our radio station in Monte Carlo. They left Trans World Radio in 1966, Ben having been invited by the National Religious Broadcasters to serve as their executive secretary.

The reason for another station and more power was simply so that we could talk to more people, so that we could cover the target areas more effectively during prime listening hours with the Gospel.

Entrance to the transmitting site on Bonaire

Bill Mial, first field director on Bonaire

Experts in the field of international radio, consultants in Geneva, Switzerland, at the University of Edinburgh, in Darmstadt, Germany, and members of the Voice of America staff—all of these were telling us we would need a transmitting spot in addition to Monte Carlo, if we were to reach our target areas more effectively. They all agreed that the best supplementary spot would be somewhere in the Caribbean area. From there you can broadcast to four of the five continents in the world with considerable effectiveness. Some of the Geneva consultants suggested I contact the Dutch authorities regarding the possibility of locating in one of the Dutch protectorates.

In Puerto Rico I discovered that, even if they granted us a permit to build a station, they would offer only two frequencies at a time. In international radio this would be somewhat like having both hands and feet tied for a cross-country race.

In the meantime, the research continued. We learned that as the sending power from Monte Carlo would begin to lessen in the evening hours, a Caribbean station—by virtue of its location—would begin coming into certain areas strongly. One station would complement the other, providing a one-two punch into any of our target areas, giving us the optimum outreach to designated areas. We found ourselves in one of the best spots in the world to increase our potential. All of the studying being done for us by competent engineers was aimed at determining the actual specifications for our new transmitters and antennas. No matter where we would settle in the Caribbean we could use this information.

Shortly after the Puerto Rico trip, while visiting our staff in Monte Carlo, I stopped to phone an old friend who was working for the Phillips Radio Company in Holland. I asked if he would arrange an appointment for me with a representative from the Netherlands Antilles or Surinam. On the strength of his suggestion I went ahead and flew to The Hague. On arriving I phoned the office of the Netherlands Antilles representative.

"I think you can do something much more helpful than see me,

Dr. Freed," the representative told me. "It just so happens that right at this time Mr. I. C. Debrot, Minister of Culture and Education for the Netherlands Antilles, is in Holland. It would be much more to the point for you to talk with him."

When I phoned Mr. Debrot he said he would be happy to see me in three or four days, but that he was leaving for Amsterdam right then. I explained that I was returning to America almost immediately, then suggested if I would come over to Amsterdam that afternoon we could talk a few minutes. He agreed.

I traveled the fifty miles to meet Mr. Debrot, and our few minutes rapidly snowballed into three hours. He became intensely interested in the possibilities of what could be done for the Antilles Islands through a super-power radio station. He saw the value that this kind of installation would have for the entire area, making the islands known throughout the world. He was readily convinced of the potential for both of us.

Ten days after I returned to the States an official cable from the Antilles government was delivered to my office. It was an invitation to come down to the islands for a preliminary conference about a station.

As the KLM jet flew into Curacao, seat of the central government of the Netherlands Antilles, I was conscious that I could not push this thing through myself. Everytime I started to move out on my own, I had to stop because of my health. I knew the Lord was directing, and that any progress would have to be His advance.

Statius Muller, director of the Information Service, met me at the airport and took me by car into Willemstad, the capital of the island. The following day we were invited to meet the government officials at a dinner meeting in old Fort Nassau, overlooking the quaint Dutch-style town and harbor.

The ministers were wonderfully helpful, and wanted me to continue technical discussions with Mr. R. H. van Haaren, head of the Department of Post, Telegraph and Telephone. Mr. van Haaren, with the backing of his government, indicated they would give us total cooperation—permission to use any number of shortwave frequencies which would not interfere with local operation, and permission to go to any amount of power in both shortwave and standard wave broadcasting. The latter came in answer to my unbelievable request for 500,000 watts, to be the most powerful AM station in the Western Hemisphere, and a frequency suitable for that much power. The strongest stations in the United States operate on one-tenth of that power—50,000 watts, so I knew I was asking boldly.

Prime Minister E. Jonckheer, Acting Lieutenant Governor Markos, and Minister of Finance Kroon were especially eager to do everything possible to make a location in Curacao attractive to us. I had intended to spend only three or four days in the Antilles in preliminary investigations. But the interest was so keen, the desire so apparent, and the arrangements so generous that I stayed on for two weeks at their request.

The TWR office and studio building on Bonaire

During that time, in individual conferences with the various ministers, and in joint sessions, a permit was drawn up that would allow us 1) to choose any workable frequency on the AM dial, 2) to go up to half a million watts of power AM, 3) to build any number of shortwave transmitters of any amount of power, 4) to use any reasonable number of frequencies, 5) to receive free from the local government a piece of property ten miles out of Willemstad to be used as the station site, 6) to use channel 2 for a television station at any time in the future.

In the presence of an eager body of Curacao government officials gathered in the main conference room of the Central Government building, Prime Minister Jonckheer handed over our official permit to build a super-power radio station.

We had conferred with several governments in the Caribbean—either we had contacted them or they had approached us—and I had expected it would take at least two years for us to reach the permit stage with any of them. It was a miracle that within two weeks after I arrived in the Antilles, we were given permission to set up a super-power station on Curacao in the Netherlands Antilles Islands.

Never before in the history of broadcasting has a private group of any kind been granted such a permit. It would enable us to reach multiplied thousands in the interior of many countries, thousands who would never ever hear otherwise.

I recall that, on returning to the United States, one of our staff men asked me, "How do you know this is God's will to take such a giant step in the Caribbean? There seems to be such a fine line between faith and foolish presumption."

"First of all," I said as I answered him, "we can't look at the cost. We must determine the will of God, then move ahead with confidence regardless of the cost, knowing that since we have conformed to His will, He will provide the means."

Is not this, after all, the crux of confident Christian living? First, to seek the will of God; then, to step fearlessly into that will.

Almost as soon as I was back in the States we began to make arrangements for the building of our transmitters, the entire antenna system, and the power plant. The equipment was to be the most modern in every way, a further refining of the systems used by Voice of America. The antennas were to be designed so they could reach in all directions with maximum power and efficiency. The transmitters were to have the latest vapor cooling system and other up-to-date modern features. We must make every technical effort to reach every person possible.

Several companies in the United States, in Holland, in Switzerland, and in Germany, were capable of handling our job, but we awarded the contract for both the transmitter and antenna system to Continental Electronics in Dallas, Texas. They already had experience building the largest broadcasting equipment in the world for Voice of America, and for other powerful stations such as those in Okinawa and Munich, Germany. The bid for the diesel power plant went to Alco-Westinghouse in Schenectady, N. Y.

"Broadcasters throughout the world are increasing both their power and numbers of hours on the air," reported Director Loomis of Voice of America. "The radio waves are filled with a multitude of voices vying for the attention of the listeners.

"The only recourse open to the VOA," concluded Loomis, "is to have more power than competitors on the same frequency, and to be more flexible in the use of frequencies. This is jungle warfare. Victory goes to the strong, the smart, and the quick."

In order to compete in this "jungle of sound"—to reach the never-dying souls of men and women with the transforming message of the Gospel—we knew we would have to match—or even surpass—the super-power of secular stations. We knew that men and women in many areas of the world would not know Jesus Christ without the multiplication of blessing possible through modern radio's super-power.

After the contracts were signed for the necessary equipment we began to question—what did we forget, what have we left out, what mistakes have we made? We had spent several months drawing up the right kind of contract with Continental Electronics and Alco-Westinghouse, and the biggest job, we found out, was the continual interaction required between Trans World Radio staff people and Continental technicians. Changes and modifications had to be made. Decisions could never be made solely on a technical basis, for they were often reached only by a constant reviewing of our missionary goals. We were indebted time and time again to our own staff in Monte Carlo, to others in Christian broadcasting, to scholars and technicians in strategic positions, who stood ready to advise and work with us.

The amazing upshot of these months of planning turned out to be how *few*—not how many—things went wrong! The major companies with whom we worked were extremely fair in their

Transmitter building on Bonaire

dealings with us. We found them honest workmen, willing to shift with us as necessary.

The entire task of coordinating and expediting the project at this end was unbelievably complex and cumbersome. I felt it was essential to secure the best help available. The man who came immediately to mind was Bill Mial, who, with his wife Joan, had done such an excellent job in assisting my father in the establishment of the broadcasting ministry in Monte Carlo. It would be difficult for me to outline fully Bill's contribution during the following year, as he and his family moved to Chatham, New Jersey, to assist in our home office and to work alongside me personally during this great forward move.

Meanwhile, in Curacao Doug and Betty Griffin had moved into one of the little houses on the property given to us by the government. Fresh from Monte Carlo and seasoned by experience on the TWR staff in Tangier as well, the Griffins worked out of their home, well-equipped to make plans for construction, check materials, and evaluate problems.

As they became acquainted with this subtropical coral island off the coast of Venezuela, they, and others of us, began to foresee serious difficulties. Engineers, both ours and the government's, looking into the intricacies of a super-power station, started to worry that we would be located too close to the jet airport in Curacao. The more we investigated, the more we became afraid of the combination. This was not only because of the problems it posed for us, but because of the possible problems that we might create for incoming planes.

About this time I heard that my friend Mr. Markos, who had been Acting Lieutenant Governor of Curacao, had just been appointed by the Queen to be Lieutenant Governor of the adjacent island, Bonaire. I began thinking that maybe it would be a good idea to look over things there. So I asked Doug to do a little exploring with me on Bonaire.

He came back all excited. There were fewer people on Bonaire than on Curacao. There was no jet airport. And the large salt flats gave us conditions that appeared to be technically superior. When I approached Mr. Markos and the leading officials of the island, they were immediately interested and receptive to the possibility of our building an immense missionary radio station there.

Although it was not easy for them to do so, the officials of Curacao were gracious in releasing us from our permit with them—at no cost to us. We had made no investment of any kind. Two weeks remained before construction was scheduled to begin. All of the planning to this point was completely transferable to Bonaire.

Curacao had been the open door for us into the Caribbean. If we had gone first to Bonaire to investigate its potential for our use, it would have looked like an impossible island to us. Only 112 square miles of coral rock, shaded by a few palm and divi-divi trees, it sits low in the waves, rising to a low mountain range at the north end. The wind blows constantly through a tropical temperature. It lies just east of Curacao, and is second in size of the Leeward Antilles group. But we discovered technically there could not be a better spot anywhere in the world—Bonaire is predominantly salt flats, with salt water on all sides, providing unbelievable conductivity, wet salt being the next best conductor to metal! Many of the experts said it was like doubling our power to put the station there.

An article in one of the Netherlands Antilles' newspapers stated, "The Central Government [of all the Antilles islands] has no objection that the permission has been granted for the erection of this station on Bonaire. Mr. R. A. van Haaren, director of Lands-Radio, visited Bonaire to look at the plans and the project. He found everything in order. The Government of Bonaire will work together as closely as possible with Trans World Radio. It is good that this transmitter stayed in the Antilles.

"There are several Bonaire workers who have found work with this project. Dr. Freed was ever so thankful for the tremendous welcome and wonderful help he found there. With his staff Dr.

Freed is completely convinced of a definite call of God to send to the world the Gospel. On the other hand, this call of God is taken on with the well-known American business-like way."

God had given us a dedicated group of men to serve on our Board of Directors. These devoted men have been the backbone of Trans World Radio throughout this entire project, as well as in the many other facets of our ministry. William Haynes, A. L. Robertson, and R. B. Turney have served faithfully on the board since the inception of Trans World Radio. Weaver Futrell, Milton G. Frazier, Paul Grube, Milton Klausmann, George W. Lynch, and James O. Buswell III have served for many years on the board. In recent years the inclusion of Leroy Webber, Milton Klausmann and John Hallett has done much to increase further the strength and vitality of the board.

The TWR Board of Directors:
left to right, first row: A. L. Robertson, William P. Haynes, Paul E. Freed, Ralph Freed, Milton G. Frazier;
second row: Weaver Futrell, Milton Klausmann, R. B. Turney, John C. Hallett;
third row: Thomas Sanders, Leroy C. Webber, George W. Lynch, Hermann Schulte, James O. Buswell III.

These men come from many walks of life. Several are pastors, others serve the Lord in the business world, while others with special talents have provided a powerhouse of leadership for Trans World Radio. Not only have they helped formulate the policies, but they have shown a tremendous desire to uphold my father and me and the entire staff in many ways. They have stood with us through both joy and sorrow, victory and defeat, in praise as well as criticism, and in the ultimate victory of God's plan and purpose. Their value can never be measured in human terms and only eternity will reveal the full effect of their dedicated guidance.

God has also given us a devoted and capable staff of workers at our headquarters in Chatham, New Jersey. In the area of administration Bob Dickinson is rendering invaluable help. He is not only talented and capable, but a man of deep spiritual commitment. Ted Bleich, our financial secretary, is a man who renders tireless and efficient service in his most vital work. He is unique in the way in which he injects a deeply spiritual tone in dealing with TWR workers and the general public in this normally technical activity.

God brought us step by step until He had moved us to the spot where He wanted us, at exactly the right time on His clock. All along the way He gave us great peace. The progress was slow and steady, and the deep calm gave us no room to doubt that we were on schedule with the Lord. Even when we would have liked to move more rapidly, we did not wonder if we were going the right direction. This was God's program, and we felt good about being a part of it.

The government officials of Bonaire made it as easy as they possibly could for us as to working out the details of building a station on their island. They gave us nearly a square mile of land outside of Kralendijk, the capital, plus an excellent piece of property in the center of town. They told us they would pave the roads and install ten phone lines between the capital, where the studios were to be built, and the transmitter site outside the city. They planned to clear the land for us free of charge, and put in landscaping and parking lots at both sites, and to deliver all the coral rock we would need. All of the radio equipment they promised to bring into the country duty-free. Better air service was immediately investigated. And the government guaranteed a loan on whatever buildings we wanted to put up.

Our TWR men Dan Harvey and Dick Olson, later joined by Jack Stoner and Bob Schultz and others, began construction under the supervision of Doug Griffin. Experienced through the stations in Tangier and Monte Carlo, Doug Griffin was confident that God would guide in this installation just as miraculously as He had in the others. The transmitter and diesel buildings were the first on the schedule. Construction began in September 1963. When the architect heard we were going to do the building ourselves, he over-designed everything. Later when he came to look at the finished product he grinned and shook his head, "You'd never get that good a job from a contractor! And besides, you're two or three months ahead of schedule."

About the same time a crew from Continental Electronics began putting in bases and feeder lines for the antennas. The AM tower, being erected to a height of 760 feet, caused many problems. At two or three hundred feet the tradewinds often blow fiercely across Bonaire at fifty to sixty knots. This created a situation so intolerable for the workmen that one crew gave up and walked off the job. Continental, looking for a hardier group of men, came up with the best in the business—a crew that had just finished a complicated installation in the Orient. With better equipment and more experience, they were able to complete the job.

When it came time for us to begin building the studio building and homes, God had another surprise for us. Gerhard Puppel, an East German Christian who had moved to the United States, had developed a successful business building fine homes in Michigan. In the prime of his business he heard the story of Trans World Radio and sold everything he had to join us in Bonaire. He and his wife have contributed generously to our getting started in the

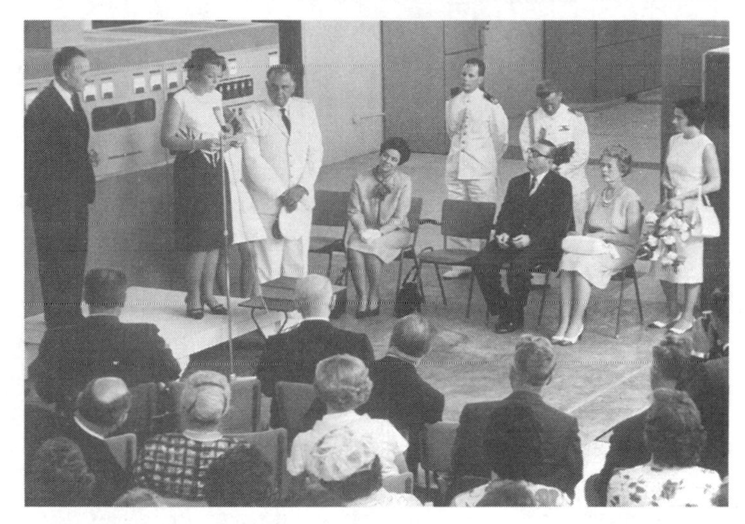

Dedication of the TWR station on Bonaire in 1964 with Crown Princess Beatrix of the Netherlands

Princess Beatrix and Dr. Freed tour the Bonaire facility

Caribbean, and their story of commitment so stirred an independent Baptist church in their home community that the members took on the entire support of the Puppels.

As we approached the time when we would begin transmitting I was bothered by one glaring problem. Earlier in the schedule we had had to select our frequency for the 500,000 watt AM transmitter. We had the choice of virtually any frequency that would not cause severe interference with the countless stations in North and South America. After much study and work we had the choice narrowed down to two different spots on the dial. At one point we finally had to pick one and stick with it, because the transmitter and the tower as well had to be built to the specifications for a particular frequency.

We felt that 800 on the dial was the best frequency under serious consideration for two reasons. First of all, there are at least three times the number of people turning to a spot in the middle of the dial than there are turning into stations at either end. Second, there is no station in the United States broadcasting at the 800 spot after sundown. In fact, it is the only frequency unused in the U. S. at night. Many other things as well made 800 kc. look favorable to us.

But there was one major problem. In Maracaibo, Venezuela's second largest city, only 150 miles away from Bonaire, there was a strong local station broadcasting with 25,000 watts of power exactly at the 800 spot on the AM dial. We were well aware of this. Also we realized that there was a friendly relationship between Venezuela and the Netherlands Antilles, as well as between Venezuela and the United States. Logically and normally this would be the last country with which we would want to interfere. But there was no question in my mind that aside from the dilemma of Maracaibo, 800 should be the right choice. Many experts strongly advised against our picking this frequency.

When I could no longer stall for time, I heard myself telling the officials that 800 would be the best frequency for us. I thought I must have lost my mind to have so thoroughly jeopardized Maracaibo, and perhaps even our relationships with Venezuela.

After the transmitters were installed—with only two weeks remaining until we would go booming down the entire length of the South American continent—something happened that we still find difficult to believe. All of a sudden we realized we were not picking up a signal anymore from Maracaibo. We thought some breakdown must have silenced them temporarily. But after several days of no broadcasting we investigated and discovered that the Maracaibo station had gone bankrupt and was off the air permanently!

Because Maracaibo kept the 800 spot open for us, we were able to move into a ready audience, with fantastic results almost immediately from Venezuelan and Colombian listeners. If we had started earlier while Maracaibo was still broadcasting, we would have overpowered their programs so severely they could have brought severe pressure on us to drop our frequency. Here again we took a step that humanly appeared foolish, yet I knew it was right. It was God's spot and God's time for us.

On October 1, 1964, we held the official opening of our powerful radio complex for top officials in the islands. Dedication of the station was held on February 25, 1965, to coincide with Crown Princess Beatrix' visit from Holland. At this time Christian broadcasters, members of the TWR board, and other friends flew into Bonaire for a two-day period of fellowship with the radio staff, which already numbered twenty-five. We were able to symbolize the outreach of the new station as we introduced to the Crown Princess a ten-year-old Bonaire girl—with a bouquet of flowers for the Princess—to represent the millions of people throughout the world who would hear the radio broadcasts from the Netherlands Antilles.

Bill Mial, who had worked so closely with me in Chatham as we planned the details of our Caribbean broadcast center, now was located in Bonaire with his family. In the important position of station manager, Bill has done a wonderful and effective job of coordinating a dedicated and talented staff.

By August of 1964 the regular AM programming was in full swing with response coming in from Canada to Tierra del Fuego on the southernmost tip of South America. Those of us who travel about the States never get over the thrill of picking up English broadcasts from "The Island of the Flamingo" as we tune our radios to 800 in Miami, Chatham, or Los Angeles. And the Spanish broadcasts literally blanket the Latin American countries to the south with the Gospel.

The big 260,000 watt shortwave transmitter began in the spring of 1965 to beam programs in many languages in every direction. With the new aids for shortwave broadcasting—high-gain curtain antennas, super-power transmitters, and computerized data — Bonaire is doing its share toward the fulfillment of Matthew 28: "Go ye therefore and teach all nations."

Since the day we decided to go with Bonaire it has been non-stop all the way!

CHAPTER XXI
SOUNDS OF LIFE

From Argentina to Canada, Cuba to India, letters come to Bonaire, bringing encouragement to station manager Bill Mial and his full-time staff, which now numbers fifty-five adults. During the first three weeks following the opening of the Antilles' radio complex, 1200 letters arrived to give evidence that the programs were being heard in fifty-eight different countries—in Europe, Africa, Central and South America, and the United States. Beginning at 4:00 A.M. each day the huge diesel engines—each one as large as a railroad locomotive—throb into action. The first program goes out in Portuguese, beamed into Brazil, then others are beamed to Central and South America in English, Spanish and Dutch; then on through the day, and up until midnight, programs in twenty other languages wing through the air at the speed of light to be caught in tiny transistor sets, clock radios, head phones, and table models around the world.

From Oslo, Norway, a twenty-one-year-old student of philosophy wrote, "I'll take this opportunity to thank you for your programs which go on the air from your newly erected radio station on Bonaire . . . through missionary radio my eyes have seen our true God."

A listener from England described the signal as "colossal . . . never heard anything like it from the Latin American area."

From Jamaica someone said, "I've been listening to your Gospel broadcasts for nine months . . . and I have now decided to serve the Lord and to put all my trust in Him."

And on nearby Curacao a listener wrote that she and a group of friends and neighbors gathered every Monday afternoon in her home. "Your programs are doing a great work," she explained, "in the hearts of many who have always lived in darkness and are now accepting Christ as their personal Savior."

On vacation in Florida a couple wrote, "We had checked into a motel early just to relax. We had asked God for a special blessing . . . and in dialing around our little transistor radio we picked up your program very clear . . . thank you for the spiritual 'life' it gave us."

Translated from the Portuguese, a letter from Brazil reads, "Every night we listen from midnight until three in the morning. For those who work all day, the night is for rest . . . but I sacrifice three hours of good sleep for the grand compensation of hearing the beautiful hymns . . . today, many friends accompany us in this joy."

"Cuban youth are very concerned about religion," writes a young man. "I can tell you this because I am a twenty-five-year-old student myself."

From Poland, "I listen daily to your broadcasts . . . the reception is good. During July my wife and I went to Russia to visit my daughter . . . People there are also listening to your broadcasts. We visited the home of a brother in Christ who has a radio . . . all his neighbors come to his house and listen with him to your broadcasts."

Another in Poland writes, "Thanks to your broadcasts, I definitely put my faith in the Lord . . . I would like to read

Gospel literature in order to tell others about Christ. I beg you please send me some."

From the Bahamas, "I am writing to tell you that plenty of people in Nassau are listening to your ministry . . . wherever you go, you will hear people talking about Trans World Radio . . . in the Bahamas any little transistor can catch Trans World Radio."

From Barbados, "I am ten years old and I would like to learn more about Jesus. Your preaching touched my heart tonight. Thank you for opening my heart to God."

From Yugoslavia, "Your broadcasts bring much spiritual comfort. I never was able to pray as I do now. You, through your broadcasts, have touched my soul deeply. I became a different person and see a definite change in my life. Please accept my sincerest thanks."

Other letters indicate that the broadcasts are heard clearly in such places as Czechoslovakia, Latvia, India, Finland, Ceylon, South Africa, Ghana, and on ships at sea. Even in Australia, there is a growing audience. Missionaries attempting to reach the masses, write to express their joy. One said, "Through this great work thousands of souls are being reached. We visit homes here in Venezuela that are completely evangelized by your powerful messages, and when we give the invitation, many of them come surrendering to Christ."

A grateful missionary from Colombia vividly told a true story to us: "After years of having the Gospel strangled here, it is such a blessing to have it beamed in every day with such clear reception. One of our Colombian pastors told me that in his town in the Guajira he could go down the street in the early hours and hear your program from almost every house. One remote area where we used to visit was visited again this past week-end and we were delighted to find one of the obstacles to the work there almost removed because the person involved is listening daily and exclusively to the excellent messages on your broadcasts."

The ministry of indigenous pastors is being supplemented and their opportunities expanded. A Colombian in Medillin wrote, "With your radio work you have actually accomplished what had previously been an impossibility for us . . . namely that of penetrating thousands of homes in this city with the Word of God . . . I have noticed that people who formerly refused to listen to us, now answer with interest saying, 'You know, I like this way they speak and the hymns they play over the Bonaire station.' "

From Paraguay, a listener writes in Russian, "You are probably unaware of what the Lord is doing through you. I have been so blessed by your programs that I just had to write . . . believers are listening and others are turning to the Lord . . . I recently baptized seven converts."

The world's population is expanding rapidly. It is expected to double by the end of this century. When Christ saw the multitudes, He was moved with compassion. Can we do less than be concerned for their eternal destiny today?

CHAPTER XXII THE PRICELESS GIFT

My five trips through Iron Curtain countries showed me firsthand some of the special difficulties we face in broadcasting. The Iron Curtain is not readily penetrated. It runs for thousands of miles across the center of the whole European continent. But God's Word can be beamed into this part of the world too—by radio waves moving at the speed of light!

I will never forget the time I was allowed to visit a collective farm near Irkutsk, Siberia, north of Outer Mongolia. The director of the farm took me on a tour of many buildings, and noted my expression of surprise as we came to a small church in excellent repair. Sensing my confusion in seeing a church on this atheistic farm, the director invited us in to look at the building. The vestibule appeared to be similar to any church entrance, but as we walked through the doors of the sanctuary, I was shocked. This place where God was once worshiped was now the farm's chicken hatchery!

The disappointment on my face made the director grin from ear to ear, "Nobody goes to church on our farm," he said laughing. "I would rather get drunk on vodka than go to church."

Later, walking through one of the humble little homes where

the workers live, my disappointment turned to hope as I noticed a radio placed in the very center of the living room. To me that radio represented the spiritual hope of the USSR. A conservative estimate figures some twenty million radio sets in the Soviet Union—at least 92 per cent with shortwave bands. This gives us the tremendous possibility of piercing the Iron Curtain for tens of thousands of radio listeners, of bringing them the message of truth and life through Jesus Christ.

With some 225 million people in the Soviet Union there is not one Sunday School! Imagine what the "Sunday School of the Air" must mean to those who listen. Christian parents are extremely grateful for the radio programs for children and youth to provide Christian training and education.

We have been in the Soviet Union several times to investigate the needs, to find out about the listening habits of the people there, and to test the radio signals we were beaming into Russia and the satellite countries. The immediate impression we gained was two-fold: 1) because of the widespread use of shortwave sets there would be no problem of an audience, and 2) people were extremely anxious to hear radio programs from the West. We had no doubt from the beginning that preparing programs for daily broadcast into Russia would be the right thing to do, no matter what it would cost in money and effort. From the earliest days in Tangier it was possible for us to go into the satellite nations in eleven different languages, and by 1960 we were well into our schedule of programs in Monte Carlo.

Now eight full-time workers in Monte Carlo are producing a wide range of Russian programs. Nick Leonovich, head of the Russian department, and his wife, Roz, are assisted by Earl and Pirkko Poysti—Earl is a native of Siberia, Paul and Betty Semenchuk from the Ukraine, and Mr. and Mrs. Paul Naidenko. Several of them have attended Christian schools in both Europe and the United States. All are capable, highly specialized workers.

Peter Deyneka, Jr., of the Slavic Gospel Association, has

commented, "I can hardly believe that a station could go into such depth of programming to fit the actual needs of the Russian people as has Trans World Radio." Russians report that the TWR staff is marvelously reaching their own people in the Soviet Union. In Moscow alone, we are told, people are listening by the tens of thousands.

There are so few Bibles available that people are tremendously hungry for Bible teaching. A minister from Russia, who came into Czechoslovakia, begged us to get him a copy of the Bible. "There are three of us preachers who go out to the villages. But between us we have only one Bible. Therefore, we have divided the Book into three parts, and we circulate the parts between us so we each have a portion from which to preach."

Thousands of letters continue to come in from behind the Iron

Nick Leonovich (center), director of the Russian department in Monte Carlo, with two Russian workers

Curtain. Many souls are being saved, Christians are being strengthened through the preaching of God's Word, and believers are being encouraged to witness actively to their faith in Christ.

A teen-ager living in Moscow recently wrote, "I am sixteen years old and a science student. Previously I bowed before the tree of knowledge, but you—through your voice—have begun to sow the seed of faith in my soul."

Another teen-ager living in East Germany comments on our recently inaugurated young people's programs beamed to that country, "I am persuaded that preaching the Gospel by radio will reach many teen-agers who have been neglected in the past. I am glad you have bridged this last gap. Many of my friends listen to your programs."

Our Russian programs also reach into many outlying areas. "Each day we leave the fields early," writes a Siberian farmer, "so we will not miss your Gospel programs. We all dress in our best clothing and gather around the radio set to worship God."

To Russian Christians these programs are like an oasis in the desert—being able to listen to the Gospel in their own language, in the privacy of their own homes, is an absolutely priceless gift.

Barriers exist in many parts of the world. Veteran missionaries agree that one of the most difficult mission fields on earth is that of Israel and the Arab lands. No Christian missionary has ever set foot in Medina, Saudi Arabia, the Holy City of Islam; but the Gospel is nonetheless proclaimed there with power and clarity by radio.

"I was greatly impressed by the program on redemption and sacrifice in relation to Christ," writes a native of Medina. "Would you kindly send me a copy of the program? Why don't you increase the length of your program, or give us more programs each week?"

A listener in Jerusalem, intimately familiar with the streets and paths that Jesus knew, wrote to us to say that he is beginning to understand the good news of God's love in Jesus Christ. "After listening for a time to your radio programs, there came a change in my mind and feelings. Please send me a whole Bible with a New Testament for I want to know more about Jesus."

Reports of conversions to the Lord Jesus Christ are received daily. A listener in Colombia writes, "There have been twenty-five persons converted to Christ by means of a radio receiver that I have. I invited them to come and listen to my radio. Now they give thanks to the Lord that they have heard and received the Word of Life."

A separate letter from this man's wife states that she was won to the Lord as she listened to Trans World Radio from Bonaire.

Missionaries in many parts of Latin America have told us that Trans World Radio plays an important part in their ministry. Radio receivers, left at distant mission stations, assure proclaiming of the Word of God even though a missionary is not present.

Reports indicate that our signal is extremely strong throughout the islands of the Caribbean including Cuba. A listener in Matanzas, Cuba, writes, "I have recommended your program to many friends, and I can tell you with sincerity that it is like a ray of light bursting through a dense cloud that encompasses my country. I always hear TWR when I arrive home from work and you cannot imagine how it reinforces me spiritually. Here in Cuba these programs arrive very well."

My father and I have often talked of the many miracles we have seen performed during the past twelve years. The world has often scoffed at God's wonderful purpose. We have often heard those doubting words, "It can't be done"—but God has done the impossible. Beginning with a dream—a vision in the hearts of men—God first provided the small station in Tangier, then the giant transmitters of Monte Carlo on the continent of Europe itself, and now the super-power equipment in Bonaire. God has indeed done the impossible!

God has also done the impossible in breaking down barriers

which man has created. Daily the light of Christ floods into the darkest corners of the earth with the lifegiving message of salvation through Jesus Christ.

It would take another book even to tell of what God is doing today through Gospel broadcasts into the Soviet Union and the other eastern European countries as well. Thousands and thousands of letters, as well as personal contacts, testify abundantly to a great surge of hungry, needy hearts turning to our Savior. We realize this is true, in a great part, because of the tremendous sacrifices made by folks around the world.

When I was in Poland, two young Christian men led me along the dusty streets of a village near Warsaw to meet a Christian widow. She lived alone in a one-room shack with none of the world's joys, but the radiance upon her face told me she was a child of the King.

When my friends introduced me as the president of Trans World Radio, she said, "Oh, I know God has sent you here. I have prayed for you a long time. I want to tell you what God has done for me."

She led me to the door and pointed down the street, "Do you see that little house over there? One evening some friends invited me to their home and had me sit down in front of a radio. For the first time in my life I heard of Jesus Christ. My boy and girl listened, too. I cannot tell you the joy we all had as we dropped to our knees at the end of the broadcast and found Jesus Christ as our personal Savior that night."

As I looked around her room at the obvious poverty and realized how difficult it must be for her, I said, "I feel sorry for you."

Her answer was simple, yet profound, "Feel sorry for me? Don't feel sorry. I'm the happiest woman on the face of the earth. I have everything—I have Jesus Christ."

As we were leaving she touched my arm and said, "There is something, however, that makes my heart heavy. Thirty million people in my country need Jesus Christ! Why is there only one little Gospel broadcast a week to thirty million people? Why only one?"

I thought the answer was obvious. "Because we do not have the money with which to put on more programs," I said.

"Ah, is that the problem? Is that the problem?"

Her face lit up as she walked to the corner of the room. I watched as she pulled a little crate from the wall. There was an envelope underneath which she picked up and brought to me.

"Here, sir, this is everything I have. Use it to broadcast more programs so more of my people here in Poland can hear of Jesus Christ as I did. Please take it."

I looked into the envelope and saw a few bills and coins. It possibly amounted to a dollar and a half. I shook my head and said, "No, I can't take this."

I knew this was everything she had, perhaps all that stood between her and starvation.

She looked directly at me, and with the dignity of a queen she said, "Sir, I am not giving it to you. I am giving it to Jesus Christ."

SELECT TRANS WORLD RADIO OFFICES AROUND THE WORLD

Trans World Radio
International Headquarters
P.O. Box 8700 • Cary, North Carolina 27512-8700 USA

CANADA
Trans World Radio Canada
P.O. Box 310
London, Ontario N6A 4W1
Canada

AUSTRIA
TWR-Vienna
Postfach 141
A-1235 Vienna
Austria

SOUTH AFRICA
Trans World Radio
34 du Plessis Avenue
Kempton Park 1619, Johannesburg
Republic of South Africa

UNITED KINGDOM
Trans World Radio
P.O. Box 1020
Bristol, BS99 1XS
England

HONG KONG
TWR-Chinese Ministry International, Ltd.
545 Nathan Road
8/F On Lee Building
Yaumatei, Kowloon
Hong Kong

INDIA
Trans World Radio India
L-15, Green Park
New Delhi 110016
India

VENEZUELA
Radio Trans Mundial de Venezuela
Apartado Postal 47
Maracay 2101-A
Estado Aragua
Venezuela

AUSTRALIA
Trans World Radio
P.O. Box 121
Balwyn, Victoria 3103
Australia

Transmitting Locations in 1994

Albania
Bonaire
Cyprus
Guam
Monte Carlo
Russia
Sri Lanka
Swaziland
Uruguay